TOOLS FOR TEACHING
Writing

DAVID CAMPOS

KATHLEEN FAD

TOOLS FOR TEACHING
Writing

STRATEGIES AND INTERVENTIONS FOR
DIVERSE LEARNERS IN GRADES 3–8

 ASCD   ALEXANDRIA, VIRGINIA USA

1703 N. Beauregard St. • Alexandria, VA 22311-1714 USA
Phone: 800-933-2723 or 703-578-9600 • Fax: 703-575-5400
Website: www.ascd.org • E-mail: member@ascd.org
Author guidelines: www.ascd.org/write

Judy Seltz, *Acting Executive Director;* Richard Papale, *Acting Chief Program Development Officer;* Stefani Roth, *Interim Publisher;* Julie Scheina, *Acquisitions Editor;* Julie Houtz, *Director, Book Editing & Production;* Jamie Greene, *Editor;* Georgia Park, *Senior Graphic Designer;* Kyle Steichen, *Production Manager;* Keith Demmons, *Production Designer*

All web links in this book are correct as of the publication date below but may have become inactive or otherwise modified since that time. If you notice a deactivated or changed link, please e-mail books@ascd.org with the words "Link Update" in the subject line. In your message, please specify the web link, the book title, and the page number on which the link appears.

PAPERBACK ISBN: 978-1-4166-1904-8   ASCD product #114051   n8/14
Also available as an e-book (see Books in Print for the ISBNs).

Quantity discounts: 10–49 copies, 10%; 50+ copies, 15%; for 1,000 or more copies, call 800-933-2723, ext. 5634, or 703-575-5634. For desk copies: www.ascd.org/deskcopy

Library of Congress Cataloging-in-Publication Data

Campos, David.
 Tools for teaching writing : strategies and interventions for diverse learners in grades 3-8 / David Campos & Kathleen Fad.
     pages cm
 Includes bibliographical references and index.
  ISBN 978-1-4166-1904-8 (pbk. : alk. paper) 1. English language—Composition and exercises—Study and teaching (Elementary)—United States. 2. Language arts—Remedial teaching. I. McConnell, Kathleen. II. Title.
  LB1576.C3138 2014
  372.62'3—dc23
                                                2014015763

23 22 21 20 19 18 17 16 15 14   1 2 3 4 5 6 7 8 9 10 11 12

To my mother, Guadalupe,
who gives me strength, confidence, and
a sense of social responsibility.

DAVID

To Mary and Tommy,
who have taught me how important it is
to love and support all children.

KATHY

TOOLS FOR TEACHING *Writing*

INTRODUCTION

The idea for this book came from our experiences working with teachers of children who struggle with writing. In our observations, we noticed that despite teachers' best efforts to teach writing, their students were not meeting the appropriate grade-level standards. In fact, recent national results reveal that most students score at a basic mastery level, far fewer students score at proficient or advanced levels, and only about a quarter of 8th and 12th grade students attain grade-level proficiency (National Center for Education Statistics, 2012). In his 2013 report on SAT and NAEP writing score results, Graham does not mince words: we have a national writing crisis on our hands. Our middle and high school students' scores reveal that they are not ready for college and are not prepared to meet the writing demands of the 21st century workplace. Graham explains:

> We have transitioned to a knowledge economy that demands higher levels of literacy and stronger communication skills for all workers. . . . The students in school today will step into a workforce that is very different from the one their parents and grandparents entered. . . . The jobs that are available now require, on average, a higher level of literacy skill than entry-level jobs did just ten or twenty years ago—and this trend is accelerating. (Graham, 2013, p. 4)

These sorts of reports (and the writing scores themselves!) worry us. We have grown increasingly concerned over students' writing performance, especially since we repeatedly found that students could not articulate the hallmarks of good writing, did not value writing as a constructive means of communication, and were rarely motivated to write.

Why do some children struggle so much with writing? We thought about this question for a long time as we reflected on our own writing abilities and found that neither of us were great writers until someone in our adult lives took the time to show us how our writing could be improved. We recognize now that we needed this assistance because we never had direct instruction during our school years on how to write. Our language arts teachers must have assumed that since we were good readers, then we would easily transition into good writers. We suspect that our teachers thought our writing ability would become standard, or maybe even exceptional, because it would invariably come to resemble what we were reading (i.e., Twain, Hemingway, Steinbeck, etc.), as if through osmosis.

We also recalled that we had teachers who told us to write with virtually no instruction whatsoever—for example, "Write a summary on what you just read" or "Write a different ending to the story with at least three paragraphs." Then, without fail, we were handed grades with comments that were far from constructive. Red ink accentuated our grammar mistakes, and comments such as "Don't be all over the place when you write," "Think harder next time," "You need to get clear," and "Don't be so careless when you write" adorned the header. How could we ever feel inspired to maximize our writing performance with such immaterial comments? No wonder we had issues with writing! Keep in mind that when teachers assign students a writing task, provide no writing instruction whatsoever, and then offer students an appraisal that has little to no applicable benefit, they fall short of teaching writing.

Those were our experiences, but what about students today? Why do so many struggle with writing? These days, students learn how to write through varied approaches (e.g., whole-language approach, Writers Workshop, cycle writing process, etc.). This leaves many to wonder why students' NAEP and SAT writing scores are so low. We believe students struggle with writing for the simple reason that it is particularly complex.

- **Writing is a lengthy process.** The writing process is not a factual piece of information that is easy to understand or a skill that can be acquired quickly in a lesson or two. Most students can typically amass most grade-level knowledge and skills through some effort, and they can demonstrate mastery of such in a relatively short period of time. However, with writing, students have to practice patience. They have to plan, organize, draft, and revise. Along with the guidance of a teacher and help from peer editors, students may have a polished essay within two weeks—provided they have uninterrupted time to work in class. This can be too much time for some students to endure, so simply giving up becomes an attractive alternative. From a young student's perspective, people are capable of speaking their minds in conversation without formally planning, organizing, drafting, and so forth. Why, then, should they be asked to oblige their ideas through a series of actions for a simple piece of writing? Many of them cannot fathom the purpose of the writing process or recognize the artistic expression of a well-crafted sentence, paragraph, or essay.

- **Writing requires incredible concentration.** Students who expect to have a polished piece of work have a responsibility to apply themselves from beginning to end, include information to meet their objective, and carry their essay through final completion, which requires a lot of close attention. Quite often, though, they get distracted, lose their train of thought, and become discouraged, especially if the instructions and expectations weren't clear to begin with. Moreover, if students are not confident in their writing abilities, they may be indecisive when it comes to putting their ideas down on paper or succumb to writer's block.

- **There are countless rules and conventions to remember.** Read the following brief paragraph and think of the sea of grammar rules that went in to crafting it:

Yesterday, my mom and I went to the mall. We went to buy my older sister some shoes. My sister could not come with us but said that she trusted us to buy the right shoes for her. When we got to the shoe store, my mom asked, "Izzy, how would these shoes work for Monica?" I started laughing. The shoes had Dora the Explorer on them. I could not stop laughing. As a joke, my mom bought the shoes and said she would return them later. When Monica opened the box she couldn't believe it. She looked scared and wanted to laugh at the same time. Just as she was about to cry, we told her it was a joke.

In this paragraph, the student demonstrates knowledge of complete sentences, direct and indirect objects, capitalization, quotation marks, sequence, punctuation, spelling rules, and a host of other conventions. That is quite a bit of knowledge to have in mind and demonstrate accordingly. If that were not enough, the final paper has to look presentable. It has to be free of smudges and eraser marks, it has to be written within the margins, the title has to be centered, and so forth. For some students, remembering all of the rules and conventions and creating a piece of writing that is presentable is no different than asking them to explain the complete work of theoretical physicist Stephen Hawking by way of an art project that looks neat!

- **There are countless writing traits that must be understood.** Students are likely to struggle with writing if they do not understand or have opportunities to develop (through intense support or individualized instruction) traits such as focus, coherence, organization, and voice. Difficulties in mastering these traits are not "unique to struggling writers, but they are much more likely than their peers to require writing instruction that is frequent, intensive, explicit, and individualized" (Dudley-Marling & Paugh, 2009, p. 3).
- **Suggestions to improve writing must be seen as a benefit and not a declaration of shortcomings.** Quite often, a helpful comment, such as "Divide these sentences into two paragraphs," can be interpreted as an insult. For some students, it is easier to abandon the assignment altogether than to endure the writing process with a steady flow of advice.

We wanted to provide readers with resources that will help them reach out to struggling writers, and this book is our attempt to do that. We know that most teachers look for lesson outlines that incorporate tips and suggestions, checklists, instructional forms, and other easy-to-use tools because their time is limited. We've found that the more practical the materials are for teachers to implement in the classroom, the better equipped they are to use them on a regular basis. For that reason, the strategies presented here can be used in lesson planning immediately; more important, they are fun activities that motivate students to learn how to improve their writing.

As former special- and general-education teachers, we are familiar with the challenges associated with teaching students with disabilities how to write. This book, however, is designed for educators who seek to provide support for students who struggle with writing, despite their teachers' best efforts. Indeed, there are many students who experience difficulty with writing. "Negotiating and coordinating basic skills, knowledge, strategies, and conventions of written language can be difficult even for skilled writers, because writing demands that students plan, generate content, organize their composition, translate content into written language, and revise and improve their initial draft. Additionally, many children are not equipped with appropriate strategies to overcome obstacles presented by written expression" (Lienemann & Reid, 2008, p. 471).

Even the most successful writing programs require creative approaches to accommodate the needs of diverse learners. Consequently, we have included tips for English language learners, struggling readers, and students with disabilities, but nearly all of the strategies—which offer a wide range of strategies and activities—can be used to accommodate the learning styles of diverse learners. In these strategies, students work cooperatively, use checklists and concrete learning tools, use graphic and visual organizers, and are afforded open-ended activities, problem-solving opportunities, and so forth.

Finally, the Evaluation Protocol and Student and Teacher Reflection Form (Appendixes C and D, respectively) are documents that serve to measure student progress and guide teachers to plan and deliver individualized instruction. Teachers will find that the evaluation materials and strategies are powerful tools that improve students' writing because of the following reasons.

They are aligned with the Common Core State Standards and NCTE Standards. We have chosen the Writing Traits model, which was developed by Northwest Regional Educational Laboratory (NWREL) in the 1980s (and which has been steadily evolving ever since) because research supports that it works. (The NWREL document *Research on Writing with the 6+1 Traits* outlines how teaching students about the traits improves the quality of their writing). We use eight traits associated with writing; these include focus, coherence, organization, development of ideas, voice, word choice, conventions, and presentation. The most current NWREL model is the 6+1 Trait Writing Model of Instruction & Assessment, and it includes the following traits: ideas, organization, voice, word choice, sentence fluency, convention, and presentation. We firmly believe, however, that children need to know the skills associated with focus and coherence. Although sentence fluency certainly incorporates elements of focus and coherence, we have unfailingly used the terms *focus* and *coherence* in our own teaching and believe that they best capture our instructional intent, especially when we emphasize the point that students' writing should have purpose and maintain a consistent point of view.

We believe that the Writing Traits model complements Writers Workshop and can be a great component of an integrated approach to teaching literacy. Others agree that the "traits fit naturally into the writing process [because] they make teaching writing more focused and purposeful" (Higgins, Miller, & Wegmann, 2007, p. 312). Additionally, the traits provide a common language that identifies good writing. Therefore, teachers, students, and parents can speak the same "writing language" as children work toward becoming successful writers (Jarmer, Kozol, Nelson, & Salsberry, 2000; NWREL, 2012).

We also believe that by learning these traits, students develop the skills necessary to write essays that meet the Common Core State Standards and appear on standardized tests. (See Figure 1.) A more comprehensive examination of Writing Traits and its alignment to the Common Core State Standards is addressed in the document *Crosswalk Between the 6 + 1 Traits and the CCSS Writing and Language*

Standards, which is located at www.educationnorthwest.org. Figure 1 shows the standards for 5th grade and how the Common Core State Standards and the NCTE standards are aligned. For a complete list of all grade levels, consult the documents previously mentioned.

They can be used in the practice of common assessments. Professional learning communities that perform common assessments have found that their collaboration and dialogue over instructional goals, coupled with a review of student data, lead to gains in student achievement (Christman et al., 2009; King, 2012; Reeves, 2004; Schmoker, 2004). Ideally, common assessments are aligned with standards, guide teachers to prioritize instruction based on individual needs, and generate discussion using a common language (Center for Curriculum Renewal, n.d.). We believe that the material included in this book deepens teachers' conversations about writing, especially when they interpret data to analyze their students' writing and use it to inform and guide their own instructional practices (Chenoweth, 2009; Martin, 2006).

Our materials lend themselves to common assessments because the evaluation protocol, reflection forms, and strategies

- Are structured with a clear purpose about what students are expected to learn.
- Yield results that serve as data analysis for groups and individual students.
- Identify students' strengths and areas that need development.
- Identify specific strategies to help students improve their writing and thus allow for differentiated instruction.
- Provide students with structured feedback on their writing abilities.
- Can be used as a summative assessment to demonstrate writing performance.

They can be used in the implementation of Response to Intervention (RTI) Tiers 1 and 2. As most educators know, RTI has seen increased attention as a tool for assessing and teaching struggling learners. Many education experts find that RTI is an efficient means to advance high-quality teaching, early intervention, and progress monitoring so students' learning needs are addressed before they develop into academic problems that require special education services (Whitten, Esteves, & Woodrow, 2009). However, despite knowing that they need to monitor and measure student learning, teachers often find it challenging to design and implement their own assessment tools because of busy schedules. As a consequence, the materials herein are an added benefit to any language arts curriculum because they fulfill the intentions of RTI. To demonstrate, let's look at a definition of RTI:

FIGURE 1 : **Alignment with the Common Core State Standards and the NCTE Standards**

Dimensions of Writing	Common Core State Standards Writing, 5th Grade	NCTE Standards
Focus	**W.5.1** …supporting a point of view with reasons and information. **W.5.1** Introduce a topic or text clearly, state an opinion… **W.5.2** Write informative/explanatory texts to examine a topic and convey ideas and information clearly. **W.5.2** Introduce a topic clearly, provide a general observation and focus, and group related information logically… **W.5.4** Produce clear and coherent writing in which the development and organization are appropriate to task, purpose, and audience.	5) Students employ a wide range of strategies as they write and use different writing process elements appropriately to communicate with different audiences for a variety of purposes.
Coherence	**W.5.1** …create an organizational structure in which ideas are logically grouped to support the writer's purpose. **W.5.1** Provide logically ordered reasons that are supported by facts and details. **W.5.2** Introduce a topic clearly, provide a general observation and focus, and group related information logically… **W.5.4** Produce clear and coherent writing in which the development and organization are appropriate to task, purpose, and audience.	
Organization	**W.5.1** …create an organizational structure in which ideas are logically grouped to support the writer's purpose. **W.5.1,2** Provide a concluding statement or section related to the (opinion, information, or explanation) presented. **W.5.3**…organize an event sequence that unfolds naturally. **W.5.3** Use a variety of transitional words, phrases, and clauses to manage the sequence of events. **W.5.3** Provide a conclusion that follows from the narrated experiences or events.	5) Students employ a wide range of strategies as they write and use different writing process elements appropriately to communicate with different audiences for a variety of purposes.
Development of Ideas	**W.5.1** Link opinion and reasons using words, phrases, and clauses (e.g., *consequently, specifically*). **W.5.2** Develop the topic with facts, definitions, concrete details, quotations, or other information and examples related to the topic. **W.5.3** Write narratives to develop real or imagined experiences or events using effective technique, descriptive details, and clear event sequences. **W.5.3** Use narrative techniques, such as dialogue, description, and pacing, to develop experiences and events or show the responses of characters to situations. **W.5.5**…develop and strengthen writing as needed by planning, revising, editing, rewriting, or trying a new approach.	

(continued)

FIGURE 1 : **Alignment with the Common Core State Standards and the NCTE Standards**
(continued)

Voice	**W.5.2** Link ideas within and across categories of information using words, phrases, and clauses (e.g., *in contrast, especially*). **W.5.3** Write narratives to develop real or imagined experiences or events using effective technique, descriptive details, and clear event sequences. **W.5.3** Use narrative techniques, such as dialogue, description, and pacing, to develop experiences and events or show the responses of characters to situations. **W.5.3** Use a variety of transitional words, phrases, and clauses to manage the sequence of events. **W.5.3** Use concrete words and phrases and sensory details to convey experiences and events precisely.	4) Students adjust their use of spoken, written, and visual language (e.g., conventions, style, vocabulary) to communicate effectively with a variety of audiences and for different purposes. 6) Students apply knowledge of language structure, language conventions (e.g., spelling and punctuation), media techniques, figurative language, and genre to create, critique, and discuss print and non-print texts.
Word Choice	**W.5.1** Link opinion and reasons using words, phrases, and clauses (e.g., *consequently, specifically*). **W.5.2** Link ideas within and across categories of information using words, phrases, and clauses (e.g., *in contrast, especially*). **W.5.2** Use precise language and domain-specific vocabulary to inform about or explain the topic. **W.5.3** Use a variety of transitional words, phrases, and clauses to manage the sequence of events. **W.5.3** Use concrete words and phrases and sensory details to convey experiences and events precisely.	4) Students adjust their use of spoken, written, and visual language (e.g., conventions, style, vocabulary) to communicate effectively with a variety of audiences and for different purposes. 6) Students apply knowledge of language structure, language conventions (e.g., spelling and punctuation), media techniques, figurative language, and genre to create, critique, and discuss print and non-print texts.
Convention		4) Students adjust their use of spoken, written, and visual language (e.g., conventions, style, vocabulary) to communicate effectively with a variety of audiences and for different purposes. 6) Students apply knowledge of language structure, language conventions (e.g., spelling and punctuation), media techniques, figurative language, and genre to create, critique, and discuss print and non-print texts.
Presentation	**W.5.6** …use technology, including the Internet, to produce and publish writing as well as to interact and collaborate with others; demonstrate sufficient command of keyboarding skills to type a minimum of two pages in a single sitting.	

Response to Intervention integrates assessment and intervention within a multi-level prevention system to maximize student achievement and to reduce behavioral problems. With RTI, schools use data to identify students at risk for poor learning outcomes, monitor student progress, provide evidence-based interventions and adjust the intensity and nature of those interventions depending on a student's responsiveness, and identify students with learning disabilities or other disabilities. (National Center on Response to Intervention, 2010)

The materials included in this book integrate assessment and intervention through 30 customizable strategies that maximize students' writing performance. As a result, teachers can use data to identify students at risk for continued poor writing performance, monitor and evaluate students' progress, and provide evidence-based interventions.

It is critical to note that student progress in the RTI model relies heavily on the continual tracking and evaluation of students' progress. It is impossible to determine which students are succeeding with Tier 1 interventions alone unless every single student's progress is closely monitored. Likewise, after Tier 2 or Tier 3 interventions are implemented, there is no way to know if a student is responding positively without frequent, objective measures of learning. With that in mind, our materials are structured in such a way that teachers can track and evaluate each student's progress.

For our strategies to work in the classroom, we made a few assumptions about users of this book. We assume the following:

- Teachers have taught their students about the writing process. We expect that students have received formal instruction on the stages of writing, which include prewriting, drafting, revising, editing, publishing, and assessing. Students should know that writing is a process that is not necessarily linear. In fact, students should recognize that their writing becomes more meaningful, clear, and concrete as they journey through the progression of writing tasks (Cooper & Kiger, 2006).
- Students become proficient writers when their teachers use, are familiar with, and endorse the principles of Writer's Workshop. In other words, students have or have had teachers who model, share, and guide writing; conference with them about their writing; encourage them to share their writing; use literature as a model of excellent writing; and demonstrate authentic reasons for writing.

- Writing is taught in tandem with reading as part of a daily language instruction program. In other words, writing is not taught in isolation. Research has consistently shown that when reading and writing are taught together, this instruction improves student achievement, fosters communication, and helps develop students' critical thinking skills (Cooper & Kiger, 2006). In addition, students apply their writing skills across the content areas, not just during language arts class. The Common Core State Standards also advocate for an integrated approach to literacy (Williams, Homan, & Swofford, 2011).
- Students are afforded instructional time to write often.
- Teachers recognize that there is no single best writing program appropriate for *all* students. They continually seek out strategies that work to improve their students' writing.
- Teachers are familiar with the Writing Traits model and are able to use the relevant terminology and characteristics in their writing instruction. The traits and their characteristics are defined in Chapter 2, the Evaluation Protocol, the Progress Monitoring forms, and elsewhere throughout this text.
- Students can and do write sentences, paragraphs, and essays, but they may struggle with developing a clear purpose for writing, creating supporting details that align with their focus, and creating purposeful patterns. In other words, our resources may not be ideally suited for students who have serious cognitive difficulties with written expressions or have a disorder that adversely affects the fine motor ability of physical writing. Rather, these materials are intended for use as a supplement to a primary writing program and geared toward students whose skills have not adequately progressed even after comprehensive writing instruction.
- The 30 strategies in this book are intended for students in grades 3–8. Writing in these grade levels is critical because it is assessed in all content areas, and this may be the last opportunity to improve students' writing abilities before they enter high school.

2

THE WRITING TRAITS

As noted earlier, we believe that the teaching of eight traits can lead to writing success. These traits are detailed throughout this chapter.

Focus

Focus is the central idea or controlling theme of a piece of writing. Many teachers know this characteristic as "sticking to the point." Student writers achieve clear focus when they know what they want to write and how they want to write about it.

Characteristics That Convey Focus

- There is a clear understanding of the audience.
- There is a clear purpose for writing. The writer understands and demonstrates his or her reason for writing about the topic.
- There is one controlling theme.
- The main points are clear.
- There is a clear perspective in the writing—which is either close-up and narrow or broad and wide-ranging.

Take a moment to look at the following two examples. In the first example, a 3rd grade student struggles with focus and also demonstrates grammatical errors common to students of that age and grade level. His paragraph lacks a clear purpose, and he does not stick to one central idea.

> **The Monster in My Closet**
>
> A monster lives in my closet. He's looks funny. They say monsters are scary but mine isn't. He sleeps during the day and comes out night when I go to bed. Whenever I talk about my monster to my little sister she gets scared. My mom yells at me to stop. Anyway my monster has super magic powers and he can do cool tricks. He'll do whatever I want if I ask him to if you spend the night at my house my monster will not come out. Maybe one day my monster will come to school with me. Every body would be scared. That would be funny.

In the next example, the same 3rd grader has revised his essay based on his teacher's and peers' feedback. It now has one controlling theme, and his purpose is to convey the point that his monster is nice. His paragraph now demonstrates a tighter focus, as well as a better use of grammatical conventions.

> **The Monster in My Closet**
>
> A monster lives in my closet. I named him Toby. Most people think monsters are mean and scary, but Toby is nice. Even though he is green and has red eyes, he's always smiling at me. He makes me laugh. He tells me stories. He always tells me what a good job I've done at school. Toby says he'll always be there for me, especially when I'm sad or I had a bad day. I think if you met Toby you'd like him, too.

Coherence

Coherence refers to the connection of ideas that support the focus. Effective student writers order their ideas so that each sentence and paragraph logically connects to the controlling theme.

Characteristics That Convey Coherence

- Coherence exists within paragraphs (sentence to sentence) and among paragraphs (paragraph to paragraph).
- The supporting details align with the focus.

- All of the paragraphs contribute important information to the overall structure of the piece of writing.
- There are no shifts in ideas that render gaps in a reader's understanding.
- There is a sense of completeness.

In the example below, a 5th grade student struggles with coherence. Note how there are shifts in her ideas, and although there are supporting details that align with the focus, the ideas are not ordered so they logically connect with the central theme.

I Want a Dog

I wish I had a dog. She would be shaggy. I'd name her Sandy. I think I deserve a dog because I'm good at school. The one thing I like about a dog is that they always wag their tail when they see you. Also, my father would like a dog because they bark at burglars. A dog is like an alarm system. My little sister would probably dress her up all the time. I would have to save her.

I think having a dog is a good idea for all families. Dogs do so many good things, like help blind people and people with disabilities. I would train my dog to help my mom because she's always asking for help.

I would put a bandana around Sandy's neck, and I would teach her to play Frisbee. It would be fun to take her to the park and watch her catch it. Sandy would be a big dog and everyone would see her and laugh when I threw the Frisbee. We would have so much fun.

I think I deserve a dog because I have been very, very, very good and I would be happy and I would start to get better grades. Also, I'd take her walking every day and that would give me exercise. The End.

Now read the revised essay. All of the writer's details align with a focus to convince her audience why she deserves a dog. There are no shifts in her ideas, and her essay demonstrates a sense of completion.

I Want a Dog

For the last two years I have begged my mom for a dog, but she always says, "We'll see." But I never get a dog. I think I deserve a dog. First, I get good grades and I do my chores as I am told. This means that I am responsible. I also save my birthday and Christmas money, so if my dog needed a collar I would buy it myself. I would be sure to feed my dog every day, walk her when she needed, and brush her hair.

Second, a dog would be a nice addition to our family. She would bark when someone is coming. We would teach her tricks and she would entertain us. Plus, when you have a dog you have someone to come home to. She would always be at our door to welcome us home.

Lastly, a dog would be my friend. I can play with her when I'm lonely. I can tell her my secrets. I can ask her for her opinion on the clothes I wear. Whenever I need a hug, my dog would always be there for me.

If I get a dog, I'll never ignore her, hit her, yell at her, or scold her. Because she is a gift to me I would always tell her that I loved her.

Organization

Organization is evident when the essay or story is written in a fashion that makes sense. In fact, organization and coherence are very similar. Writing that has good coherence has related ideas grouped in sentences and paragraphs that convey a consistent point of view. Organization is about the arrangement of those sentences and paragraphs so they are linked logically around the writer's central idea. Hammill and Larsen (2009) explain, "Failure to plan what is to be written results in a lack of topic sentences, ineffective paragraph development and sequencing, and few related summaries and conclusions. Obviously, if a written piece is disorganized, its meaning will be distorted and perhaps lost entirely" (p. 45).

Characteristics That Convey Organization

- There are purposeful patterns of thought (e.g., narrative, expository, etc.).
- The sequencing of thought (sentence to sentence and paragraph to paragraph) is a logical progression.
- There is evidence of an organizational strategy (e.g., spatial, chronological, problem/solution, cause/effect, compare/contrast, order of importance, etc.).

- There is a meaningful introduction and conclusion by way of dialogue, imagery, analogy, anecdote, quote, question, or hook.
- There are strong and meaningful transitions.
- Information is conveyed in a manner that makes sense.

Two essays follow. In the first, a 7th grade student struggles with organization as she writes about a woman she admires. Take note of how some of the paragraphs do not demonstrate a logical thought progression. Even though she may have a purposeful pattern (e.g., her thoughts are arranged in order of importance), her writing is weak. Additionally, her introduction, choice of transition words, and conclusion are relatively simple. Although understanding is not entirely lost, the essay fails to demonstrate strong organization.

Jane Goodall: The Woman I Admire Most

I thought for a long time about the woman I admire most and I think that person is Jane Goodall. I saw a show about chimpanzees on the Discovery Channel and I learned how similar they are to humans. I think it's so cool that we learned all that from a woman by the name of Jane Goodall. There are many women who inspire us, but Jane Goodall inspires me most. You have to give her a lot of credit because she is 79-years-old and she is still doing activism work and she's done so much with her life.

First, I admire Jane Goodall because she has determination. She was determined to study chimpanzees and she didn't let anything stop her. Her father gave her a toy chimp when she was a little girl, and that may have something to do with the fact that she was interested in chimps. She was always a little crazy about animals. I'm like that, too. I have cats, dogs, hamsters, and fish. Maybe I'll grow up to study animals like Jane Goodall. Anyway, she went to Africa to study chimpanzees because a famous anthropologist by the name of Louis Leakey told her it was a good idea.

The second reason that I like Jane Goodall is because she looks like a nice person. I saw a lot of pictures of her and she just reminds me of an old grandmother who wants to hug you. I know that she cares a lot about chimps, and she cares a lot about animals, that she wants to protect them all the time. That shows that she cares. I know a lot of people who care about animals, but Jane Goodall really cares about them because she spent so many years caring for them.

The third reason I admire Jane Goodall is because she started lots of organizations. I read that there are thousands of people doing great things because of Jane Goodall. We have a Roots & Shoots club at the library but I never go to the meetings. But now I will because I know what they're all about and that's about trying to do good things with the environment. You have to give her a lot of credit for inspiring so many people to want to take care of animals and environment.

In conclusion, Jane Goodall is a remarkable woman. No wonder so many people think that she's great. Maybe one day I'll meet Jane Goodall and I'll thank her for everything she's done for us. Way to go Jane!

The final version of the essay below demonstrates a pattern of thought that is more purposeful. The writer organizes her thoughts in order of importance, and she provides a meaningful introduction and conclusion. Overall, her ideas are organized in a way that makes much more sense.

Jane Goodall: The Woman I Admire Most

Imagine leaving home at a young age and heading for the jungles of Africa to study wild animals. That's what Jane Goodall did, and whenever I think about her I'm inspired. So many of the great women we have studied this year inspire me to work for good grades, listen to my teachers, read, and do my homework. But Jane Goodall motivates me most all because she has done so many amazing things with her life.

After working as a secretary for the famous anthropologist Louis Leakey, Jane Goodall left England and went to the Gombe Stream National Park in Africa to study chimpanzees. I admire that she could leave a comfortable home and live in a tent and sometimes in the open forest for years with no entertainment like a TV, an iPad, or magazines. After all, it would get pretty boring if you had nothing to do. I think it's awesome that Jane Goodall didn't think about what she left behind. She only thought about one thing and that was her work with chimpanzees. In all of those years, Jane Goodall learned so much about chimpanzees' social and family life.

All of what Jane Goodall learned she put into words in such a caring way. I admire that she's written so many books about her experiences because it shows that she cares enough to share her knowledge with the world. I only looked at three books and in them she talks about the chimpanzees like if they were her family. Even though so many of the chimpanzees look the same to me, Jane Goodall can tell them apart. I think that shows how much she cares about them. She doesn't just see them as some animal she's studied but a family member or friend who teaches her things about life. When I start working, I hope that I will be caring, too.

Lastly, Jane Goodall's work didn't just stop with the chimpanzees and writing books about her experiences, she is a longtime animal and environmental activist and conservationist. I think it's so cool that she works to inspire others to protect animals and our environment. She's been a great leader in starting organizations, such as Roots & Shoots, that work to support animals, people, and the environment. Just think of all those people who volunteer to make this world better, all because of one person.

In conclusion, Jane Goodall is the person I admire most. She says, "It was because the chimps are so eye-catching, so like us and teach us so much that my work was recognized worldwide." Really, we recognize Jane Goodall's work because she was determined to fulfill her goals, she is caring in many ways, and she inspires others to look out for animals, the environment, and people. I hope that I can become a Jane Goodall one day.

Development of Ideas

Writers deepen their readers' understanding of the work through ideas that reveal depth of thought and substance.

Characteristics That Convey Development of Ideas

- The writer uses literary devices—such as figurative language, imagery, suspense, and dialogue—effectively.
- The writer adds, deletes, combines, and rearranges sentences and details to elaborate on his or her ideas.
- The writer effectively uses sentence variety (e.g., length and structure, rhythm, cadence, fragments, compound, compound/complex, simple, etc.).

After reading a story about Día de los Muertos, a class of 4th graders made a skeleton and were each then assigned to write a paragraph about how it would entertain the crowd at an evening party. In the first example below, there are no literary devices employed. Though some could argue that the sentences reveal a form of cadence, they are simple, nonetheless.

My Skeleton Marco

My skeleton's name is Marco. As you can see he is a cowboy just like the Lone Ranger. He wears a big hat. He has shiny boots. He rides his black horse and his name is Jay Zee. At the party Marco shows people the tricks he can do. He rides on the back of the horse. He lassos some bad guys. Everyone claps. He jumps on the roof. He lands on the hay. And then he yells, "Happy Día de los Muertos."

In the second example, the student uses several literary devices and has variety among his sentences.

My Skeleton Rico

My skeleton is a famous dancer. He likes Beyonce, Lady Gaga, and JT. He snaps his fingers and twirls around. With his black suit and hat, he is so handsome that all the girls want him to dance with them. Swish, swish, swish. Rico moves from one girl to the next like a honey bee. They all say, "Suave!" They ask, "Who is that charming skeleton in the tuxedo?" But Rico never opens his mouth. He just gives each girl a rose and smiles. When the dance is over, Rico climbs on his magnificent horse and says, "Happy Día de los Muertos! I'll see you next year!" Everyone is amazed with my dancing skeleton.

Voice

Voice is what makes a writer's style unique. Convictions and feelings are evident through the writer's choice of words. Spandel and Stiggins (1997) explain that voice is the "liveliness, passion, energy, awareness of audience, involvement in the topic, and a capacity to elicit a strong response from the reader" (p. 45).

Characteristics That Convey Voice

- The writer's voice is authentic and engages the reader.
- The writing demonstrates that the writer cares about the topic.
- There is a unique perspective.
- The writer's voice is based on an understanding of his or her purpose and audience.
- The writer uses two modes of voice: active (the subject is the doer) and passive (the subject is the receiver of the action).
- Enhanced vocabulary, such as the effective use of vivid verbs (e.g., *strong, striking, energetic, active*), is used throughout the writing.

Here are two essays from a 6th grade student. As in previous examples, the first essay is a draft, which does not convey good voice. The teaching objective here was for students to write a narrative relating a personal experience. The teacher asked students to write about what they learned about themselves during the previous year. Take a look at the first example and identify how and why it has a weak sense of voice.

I Am an Explorer

I've learned a lot about myself this last year. I didn't know that I liked suicide soda, I didn't know that I could make wheelies with my bike, and I didn't know that I could put 15 grapes in my mouth. But the one thing that I'm really, really, really surprised to learn about myself this last year is that I'm an explorer. Yes, you read that correctly, an explorer. Lots of people, even my own family, think that I'm just collecting junk when I'm in the field behind my house, but really I'm exploring. My dad says there are 500 acres back there and in ten years they will build more houses, but for now it's kind of vacant. There are so many different trees, shrubs, rocks, tall grasses, insects, and animals mostly deer.

Here's what I do. I first get my things together. I sometimes take water. I sometimes take my mom's cell phone. If a fox were to bite me I would need a cell phone. Then, I break through a crack in my back yard fence. It broke when my dad hit it with the lawn mower. He says he doesn't have time to fix it. Then, I go past the crack.

I take the trails that the deer have made. I guess they're looking for food and that's why they're back there. I once saw two deer. One time I got really scared because I saw a brown fox. It was walking fast. It stopped and looked at me. I walked away and it followed me, but then I yelled at it and it took off. I thought it was going to bite me. Then I keep walking to this huge oak tree. It's really old. I mean really old. I climb it. I was up there when I noticed a pond.

When I got to the pond I noticed fish, lily pads, cat tails, and once I saw some cranes. I think they were there temporarily because they fly to the coast. Once I heard something near my feet and I got super scared because I thought what if it's a snake. Those kinds of snakes are poisonous. It's quiet at the pond. You can't hear cars, kids, or anything.

So, the number one thing that I learned about myself is that I can be an explorer too. Maybe one day people will learn about how I discovered this land and they'll name it after me.

Now read the revised essay. Take a moment to discern what makes this example stronger than the first by answering these questions: Is this essay more engaging than the first? Is there evidence that the author cares about the topic? Is there a unique perspective?

I Am an Explorer

We have read about famous explorers like Christopher Columbus, Amerigo Vespucci, Hernán Cortés, and Lewis and Clark. For a long time I thought explorers had to be from a long time ago and they were all dead. But one thing I learned about myself this year is that I am an explorer, too. I thought you needed to have an ancient map, be on a mission for a great country, and have a huge sailboat filled with brave men who would follow my orders. But I learned that I could explore the vacant fields behind my house because there are so many things there that have not been discovered. It is a real treasure for me to explore those fields.

At first, I thought there were creepy monsters, werewolves, and zombies that lived in those fields. That sort of stuff scares me, so I stayed away. But then I got older and less scared, and I wanted to explore what was there. I slowly squeeze through a small crack in my back wooden fence. I take my notebook and draw a map of the surroundings. I always take water to keep hydrated, and sometimes I take my mom's cell phone just in case. I've made my own tracks, but I use the trails made by deer, too. I prefer to use the deer trails because there is no thorny brush to get in my way and cut me.

The first place they take me to is a huge oak tree I discovered. I think it's at least 200 years old. I like to climb it to enjoy the view. You can see ravines, dry creek beds, and tall grasses from up there. When I'm on the thickest branch, I pretend that I'm on the tower bridge of a magnificent castle. Sometimes I sit on the lowest branch and other times I jump on it to make it sway. When I was up there I saw a pond that I could explore too.

When I got to the pond it was amazing! There are beautiful cat tails and lily pads. Once there was a beautiful white flower on a lily pad. I thought about picking it but was worried that the water was not shallow. Tiny fish swim there too. I don't know if they are minnows or tadpoles, but they are so cool. I saw some white birds there once. I think they were cranes that had stopped there on the way to the coast. I thought, "Wow, those birds are amazing." One time a heard a whish in the water near me and didn't see what it was, but I got scared because I thought maybe it was a water snake. The pond is my favorite spot to go to because it is so tranquil. I can't hear cars or anyone, just the wind blowing.

I still have a long way to explore as long as I can make it past my favorite spots, the magnificent oak tree and peaceful pond. There are so many animals, insects, birds, and plants that I want to discover and draw onto my map, but I just have to be patient and remember that the ancient explorers didn't discover their lands in a day or two. I never thought that I would be an explorer.

Word Choice

A good writer uses rich and precise language in a functional way that enlightens and engages the reader. Strong word choice can expand and clarify ideas, create strong images that connect the reader to the writing, and guide the reader to a new understanding of the topic.

Characteristics That Convey Strong Word Choice

- The writer chooses the right words and phrases for the mode of writing (e.g., descriptive, narrative, persuasive).
- The writer uses words and phrases to create meaning and engage the reader.
- The writer strategically places words and phrases for a desired emphasis.
- The writer uses words and phrases for originality.
- The writer uses connotative and/or denotative words.
- The writer uses active verbs.

In the examples below, the student was asked to write an imaginative story that develops interesting characters. For the assignment, the teacher asked students to fine-tune one paragraph that described one character. This story is about a new student named Rodrigo who does not fit in at his middle school, and the writer is attempting to explain why. In the first example, note how the writer's choice of words does little to create meaning and engage the reader. Words and phrases don't appear to be strategically located, and there are few to no words that make for an original paragraph.

Rodrigo the Misfit

Even though all the dumb girls thought Rodrigo was cute, for some reason Mariah was scared of him. He was like the other boys, and he had nice hair. "He'd look better if he would cut it so that no one would think he was a girl," she thought. Everybody thought he was giving them a mean look, but really he needed glasses. Also, he always wore clothes that were too big for him. They had been his older brother's clothes. Even when it was cold outside he never wore a jacket. Mariah was beginning to believe that Rodrigo was poor.

Now read the revised paragraph. Notice how the writer's choice of words engages the reader, and there are now words and phrases strategically placed to create and enhance meaning.

Rodrigo the Misfit

All the foolish girls thought Rodrigo was adorable. But when Mariah first saw Rodrigo, she was instinctively afraid of him. He looked like a normal 8th grade boy. He was average height like the other boys, and his hair was a shaggy blonde. "If it gets longer he'll look like girl. He'd look cuter if he'd cut it short," she thought. He had a perfect shade of blue eyes, but he must have needed glasses because he squinted all the time. Most of the students thought he was giving them a mean look and would avoid him, but Mariah was smarter than they were. She also noticed his clothes seemed too big for him. "Were they hand-me-downs?" she wondered at times. He didn't even wear a jacket when it was cold outside. All of this led Mariah to confirm her suspicions—Rodrigo was poor.

Conventions

The term *conventions* refers to the mechanics of writing—spelling, punctuation, capitalization, grammar/usage, and paragraphing (NWREL, 2012). Successful writers know when and how to use appropriate conventions. Students who understand the conventions spell high-frequency words correctly; apply standard spelling strategies; apply structural aspects of phonemes, diphthongs, and so forth; and use punctuation and capitalization rules effectively (Hammill & Larsen, 2009).

Characteristics That Demonstrate Appropriate Application of Conventions

- The writer knows the punctuation rules associated with each of the four kinds of sentences.
- The writer uses the comma, the colon, the semicolon, quotation marks, and the apostrophe correctly.
- The writer knows there are rules that predict a general structure of spelling.
- The writer knows there are words that do not follow typical spelling rules.
- The writer uses mnemonic devices and other strategies to develop his or her spelling ability.
- The writer recognizes and corrects run-on sentences.
- There is subject-verb agreement in the writer's written work.
- The writer uses verb tenses correctly.

The 8th grade examples that follow represent a draft and a revision of a student's critique of a current movie. As you read this review, you will find numerous grammatical errors (not to mention that the student has difficulty with other writing traits), but the teacher decided to focus her instructional attention on the student's tendencies to write run-on sentences and avoid using commas.

The *Dallas Buyers Club* Movie Review

I saw *Dallas Buyers Club* this weekend with my mom. I thought the movie was going to be about a club in Dallas where people who buy stolen things like ipads flat screens or play stations for really cheap and get away with it but that's not what it was about. Before watching it my mom told me that it was going to be about when AIDS first began and people with AIDS began to die because there was no cures and no medicines for them. At first the movie was slow I mean really slow. They say Matthew McConaughey is a good actor and he is but the movie was slow and I just couldn't get into it. Jared Leto dresses like a woman and wants to be a woman and he becomes a friend to Matthew McConaughey. He's really believable too at first he gets on your nerves but then later you feel sorry for him. If you want to learn how Matthew McConaughey starts a club so that people with AIDS can buy medication and how Jared Leto is dying of AIDS then watch the movie. Just be prepared because it is really slow and it's kinda cool to see how everyone dressed in the 1980s. They look hilarious. The movie might be fun for you just for that reason.

The teacher conferenced with the student and gave him feedback on how to improve the review. She told him to think of the comma as a device to remind readers where to breathe. Moreover, she explained that a complete sentence should incorporate an individual thought. She encouraged him not to ramble in his writing with too many thoughts in one sentence. He was instructed to revise the draft by inserting a comma between items in a series, and using commas before *and* and *but* when he has two independent thoughts. His second draft follows.

The *Dallas Buyers Club* Movie Review

I saw *Dallas Buyers Club* this weekend. I thought the movie was going to be about a club in Dallas where people buy stolen electronics like iPads, flat screens, or Playstations. Before watching it my mom told me that it was a buyer's club for people with AIDS who could buy medication. I thought the movie was slow. Matthew McConaughey is an excellent actor, but I just couldn't get into the movie because it was slow. Jared Leto is a coactor. He has AIDS and wants to be a woman. He becomes a friend to Matthew McConaughey. In his role he's really believable. At first his character gets on your nerves, but then later you feel sorry for him. Watch this movie if you want to learn how Matthew McConaughey starts this club so people with AIDS can buy medication and how Jared Leto is dying of AIDS. Be prepared to be a little bored because the movie is really slow. A nice feature of the movie is that it is cool to see how everyone dressed in the 1980s. They look hilarious. The movie might be fun for that reason.

Presentation

Presentation refers to the appearance of the essay in actual form, on paper. Essays that demonstrate good presentation look neat—as if the student thoughtfully arranged the paragraphs, sentences, and graphics (if appropriate) and was careful to have few smears, eraser marks, and so forth.

Characteristics That Demonstrate Standard Presentation

- The writer uses a heading that fulfills the standards of the district (e.g., title, byline, name of the school, etc.).
- The writer uses appropriately sized margins.
- The writer uses minimal smears and/or traces of eraser marks.
- The writer uses few (or no) deletion and insertion marks.
- The writer uses—if appropriate—graphics that complement the essay.

In Figures 2.1 and 2.2, a 3rd grade student writes a brief paragraph about what she did over the weekend with the classroom teddy bear. At first glance, the presentation of the draft copy looks sloppy and seems to have been written carelessly, which can deter her peers from reading it at all.

FIGURE 2.1 : Student's First Draft

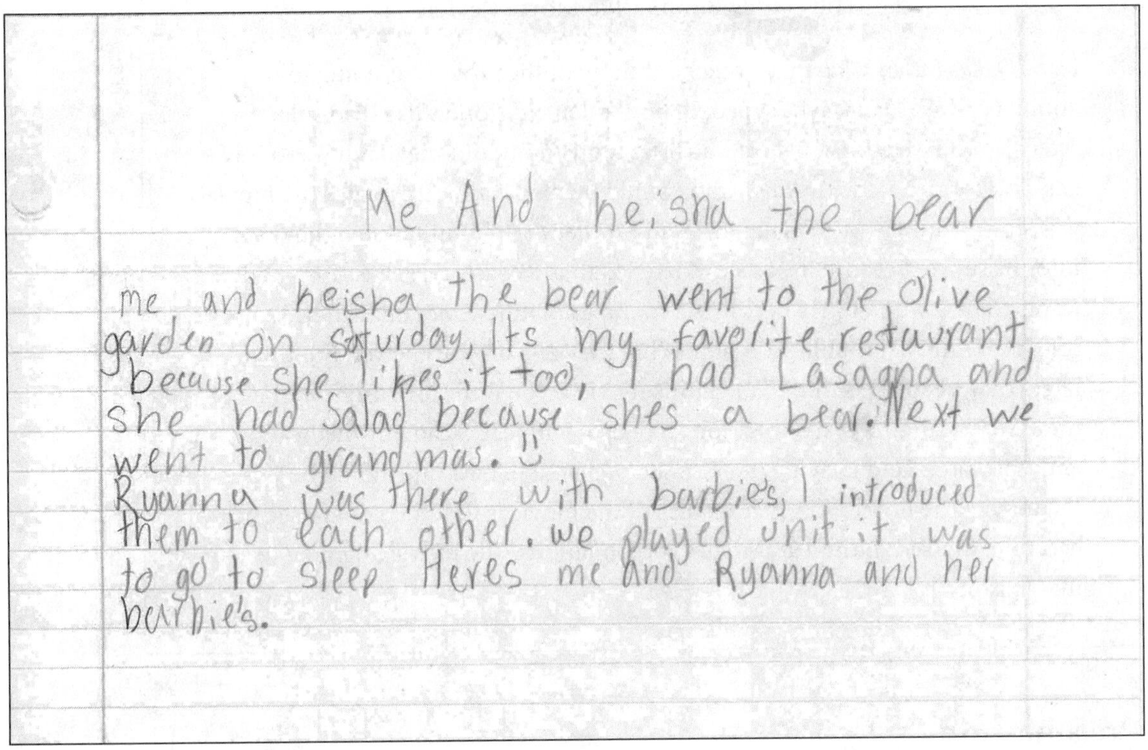

> Me And heisha the bear
>
> me and heisha the bear went to the Olive garden on saturday, Its my favorite restaurant because she likes it too, I had Lasagna and she had Salad because shes a bear. Next we went to grand mas. :)
> Ryanna was there with barbie's, I introduced them to each other. we played unit it was to go to sleep Heres me And Ryanna and her barbie's.

Source: Student work used with permission.

After consulting with her teacher and peers, the student revised the piece and fixed the mechanical errors. In her final draft, the presentation is inviting and welcomes readers with a good impression.

FIGURE 2.2 : Student's Revision

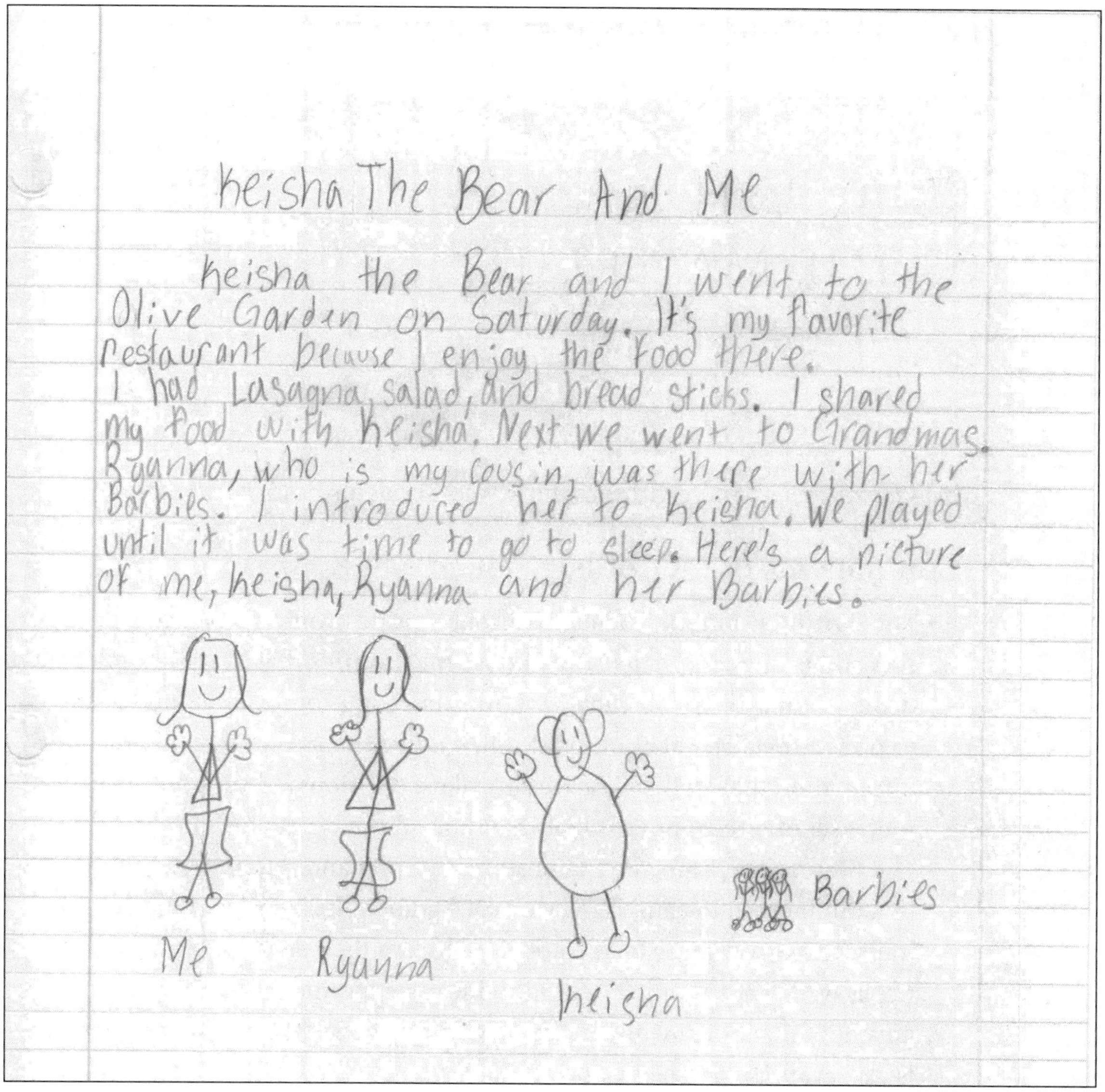

keisha The Bear And Me

keisha the Bear and I went to the Olive Garden on Saturday. It's my favorite restaurant because I enjoy the food there. I had Lasagna, salad, and bread sticks. I shared my food with keisha. Next we went to Grandmas. Ryanna, who is my cousin, was there with her Barbies. I introduced her to keisha. We played until it was time to go to sleep. Here's a picture of me, keisha, Ryanna and her Barbies.

Barbies

Me   Ryanna

keisha

Source: Student work used with permission.

3

DIRECTIONS FOR USING THE MATERIALS

Tools for Teaching Writing includes the key components described below:

Components of the Tools

- **The Writing Prompts:** There are various writing prompts that can be used as pre- and posttests. Teachers can choose the prompts that best meet their students' unique needs: prompts with illustrations, prompts that urge students to provide details and examples in their writing, and prompts that include information that students can use to take a position and support their opinion. A set of directions is available for the administration of the tests.

- **The Evaluation Protocol:** The protocol is a pre- and postassessment measure that can be used to gauge how well each student has mastered the writing traits. Teachers can use the protocol to discern their students' writing abilities as well as plan for instruction to improve specific skills. The protocol is a great tool that documents students' writing achievements. A set of directions is also available for the protocol.

- **The Student and Teacher Reflection Form:** This form can be used to reflect on a student's writing. Specifically, we ask that teachers think about what student data indicate about students' writing and make note of any areas that need attention. All data should be shared with students in a conference-like meeting. The form includes space for students to write a statement that reflects a self-assessment of their writing.

- **The Strategies:** There are 30 strategies that can be used to teach the writing traits and enhance students' writing performance so they can exceed state and national standards. Each strategy is prefaced by a brief introduction and includes a rationale that explains how the strategy can be used in the classroom. We've also provided alternatives and accommodations for students in need of additional support to complete the assignment. Instructional forms follow each strategy.

- **The Strategies Matrix:** The matrix demonstrates how all 30 strategies are aligned and linked to six of the writing traits. The six writing traits addressed by the strategies include focus, coherence, organization, development of ideas, voice, and word choice. These traits are linked to the Common Core State Standards and NCTE standards. Convention and presentation, which involve the mechanics and appearance of writing, often do not require the same degree of instruction as the other six traits. Specific instructional strategies related to these two traits are found in Chapter 5.

- **Progress Monitoring Forms:** There are two progress monitoring forms for each of six traits addressed by the writing tools. Students write a paragraph or essay directly onto the student form, and the teacher form is used to conference with the student. The forms document evidence of the specific trait.

- **Tools to Clarify Convention and Presentation:** Because most concepts associated with convention and presentation are directly taught in language arts programs (and included in most textbook teacher's editions), we have included some tools that can be used to reinforce these concepts. These include rules associated with conventions (which can be provided to students) and editing checklists.

- **Parent Resources:** A letter for parents is included that informs them of their child's performance on the pre- and posttests, your evaluation, and a description of the writing traits, along with recommendations for home activities that reinforce classroom instruction.

Directions for Use

Step 1. Collect student writing. Administer a pretest using a developmentally appropriate prompt. Use the one provided in Appendix A or display a drawing or illustration for students to view or read. Allow up to 30 minutes for students to write about the prompt. Follow the Directions for Administering the Writing Prompts, found in Appendix B.

Step 2. Read students' essays and use an Evaluation Protocol (Appendix C) to evaluate their writing. Decide whether each student demonstrates mastery of the writing traits by placing a check mark in the *yes* or *no* column beside the appropriate item(s) under each trait. Ideally, the protocol should be photocopied onto 11″ × 17″ paper so it is a booklet, and the pre- and postmeasures (i.e., the essays) can be kept within. Directions for using the protocol appear on the form. After collecting students' essays, read them carefully.

Step 3. If your evaluation of the student's writing indicates that he or she has not mastered a specific trait on the pretest, check the *no* box beside the corresponding item(s). In the "Strategy" column, specific interventions are listed and can be selected to address each item designated with a *no* (i.e., the student has not mastered that characteristic). To view the complete list of 30 strategies aligned with the writing traits, see Figure 4.0 on page 35.

Step 4. As you design your language arts lesson plans, decide which strategies to implement. There are a minimum of two strategies and a maximum of seven per pretest item. Your instruction should be differentiated based on each student's strengths and needs. For some students, you may need to implement all of the strategies linked to an item; other students may master the trait after you have taught only one strategy. Likewise, the strategies can be used for whole-group, small-group, or individualized instruction, depending on the skills of your class as a whole.

Step 5. Conference with the student using the Student and Teacher Reflection Form (Appendix D). During the conference, review the student's essay, describe what the student data indicate about the writing, identify your concerns, and write a formative critique of the writing. Be sure to emphasize some positive qualities. Have the student write his or her own formative critique of the writing. Share your review with parents by sending home a copy of the completed form.

Step 6. Read and review the strategies you selected. Then implement them according to your lesson plans, using the vocabulary of the writing traits (i.e., *focus, coherence, organization, development of ideas, voice, word choice, convention, presentation*). Some of the strategies require specific materials or a student writing sample as a basis for the lesson. Be sure to read each strategy thoroughly before teaching a lesson that includes it. We recommend implementing the strategies over a three-month period.

Step 7. We believe that students' writing improves with guided practice and constructive feedback. Providing students with numerous opportunities to write not only allows teachers to measure progress but also allows students to practice the skills targeted by each strategy. As you implement the strategies, plan to monitor students' progress continually. To do so, gather writing samples as often as possible.

Ask students to write about a topic of your choice that is developmentally appropriate. We recommend using an engaging topic suggested by a digital picture, magazine photo, postcard, or trusted online source (http://thewritesource. com/writing_topics has a great list of writing topics divided by grade level).

There are two progress monitoring forms—a teacher form and a student form—for each of six traits. (These can be found in Appendix E.) Select the form for the appropriate trait (i.e., the one with which the student is struggling), and have the student write his or her paragraph or essay directly onto the student form, reflect on the trait's characteristics, mark off the strategies used, and write a sentence about what he or she likes most about the composition. Use the teacher form to conference with the student about aspects of the writing sample you found appealing or concerning.

We advise you to create one file or binder per student and assemble all the relevant forms in chronological order. This can then be considered the student's writing portfolio. After students have used the strategies to address a specific issue, acquire another writing sample from the same student and use a new progress monitoring form. This process, when repeated, allows you to monitor each student's progress toward improving the selected writing trait.

Step 8. After completing the selected strategies, administer a posttest using one of the prompts found in Appendix A. Allow students a minimum of 30 minutes to write about the prompt. Follow the Directions for Administering the Writing Prompts (Appendix B). After collecting the students' essays, read them carefully. Decide whether each student demonstrates mastery of the writing traits, and place a check mark in the *yes* or *no* column beside the appropriate characteristics. If the student's writing has not improved (i.e., one or more *no* boxes are checked on the posttest), then you have several options for additional support:

- Reteach selected strategies using different examples of writing.
- Provide additional practice after reteaching.
- Provide additional instruction in an individualized or a small-group format.
- Review the Alternatives and Accommodations section for each of the strategies, and implement any that you have not already tried.

Step 9. Share students' writing with peers and parents, and celebrate their successes!

Matrix and Instructional Strategies

This chapter is composed of 30 strategies that can be used to support students who struggle to develop the writing traits concerning focus, coherence, organization, development of ideas, voice, and word choice. (Chapter 5 is composed of materials designed to improve students' understanding of writing conventions and presentation.) Each instructional strategy comes with

- A rationale.
- Step-by-step directions for teaching.
- Helpful tips.
- Differentiation ideas for students who need additional support, such as English language learners, struggling readers, and students with disabilities.
- Instructional forms that students use to improve their writing.

After students have written their essays in response to one of the prompts found in Appendix A, use the Evaluation Protocol (Appendix C) to decide whether each student demonstrates mastery of the writing traits by placing a check mark in the "yes" or "no" column next to the appropriate characteristics. When a student hasn't demonstrated mastery of a specific trait, select the strategies to implement during language arts instruction. The matrix in Figure 4.0 shows how each of the strategies are linked to the characteristics of six writing traits.

> Select forms, checklists, and reproducibles from this book can be downloaded at
>
> www.ascd.org/ASCD/pdf/books/CamposFad2014.pdf
>
> Use the password "ASCD114051" (no quotes) to unlock the files.

FIGURE 4.0 : Writing Strategies as Linked to Six Writing Traits

Each of the six writing traits can be found at the top of the matrix below. Under each trait are four numbers (1–4), which represent the characteristics of that specific trait. The characteristics are described in Chapter 2 and are the items on the pre and posttest measures of the writing protocol (Appendix C). The check marks under each number indicate that the associated strategy targets that specific characteristic. After examining each student's pretest measure, teachers can select specific strategies for individual students. For whole-group intervention, select the strategies that meet the needs of the group.

Strategies	Focus				Coherence				Organization				Development of Ideas				Voice				Word Choice			
	1	2	3	4	1	2	3	4	1	2	3	4	1	2	3	4	1	2	3	4	1	2	3	4
1. 3-2-1		✓			✓																			
2. Check Yourself			✓		✓		✓								✓									✓
3. Color Coding for Consistency					✓	✓																		
4. Editing Irrelevant Information			✓																					
5. Figurative Language Cards															✓									
6. Flying High						✓			✓		✓													
7. Give Acting a Shot				✓													✓	✓	✓	✓				
8. Graphic Organizers							✓	✓	✓	✓														
9. Let the Senses Help													✓	✓					✓	✓		✓	✓	
10. Listen to It																	✓	✓	✓	✓				
11. Magnifying Glass	✓																							
12. My Main Purpose			✓								✓											✓		
13. Plan It Out									✓			✓	✓		✓									
14. Prewriting Pyramid	✓		✓						✓		✓													
15. Questions to Clarify	✓	✓					✓		✓															
16. Revision Strips													✓	✓	✓						✓	✓	✓	✓
17. Rich Language Generator													✓	✓							✓	✓	✓	✓
18. Sentence Search															✓	✓								
19. Sequence Cards					✓	✓		✓	✓		✓													
20. Soccer, Anyone?	✓				✓			✓			✓													
21. Speech Bubbles																	✓		✓	✓		✓	✓	
22. Spin Your Point of View						✓			✓									✓						
23. Split Voice									✓								✓	✓	✓	✓				
24. Stick to the Point	✓		✓	✓																				
25. Three Tab POV						✓												✓						
26. Topic Sentence Development		✓				✓																		
27. Transitions Book							✓		✓		✓						✓							✓
28. Transitions Spinner										✓														
29. Vocabulary Line-Up																					✓	✓	✓	✓
30. Word Stars																					✓	✓	✓	✓
Total	5	3	3	4	3	4	3	6	7	3	6	3	4	3	3	2	6	5	5	5	5	6	6	6

Strategy 1: 3-2-1

Good topic sentences are crucial for explaining the main idea of a story or essay. Of course, well-developed topic sentences are also essential components of each paragraph within a story or an essay. Some students tend to write poor topic sentences because they write what first comes to mind and, quite often, their ideas are not well connected or organized. This strategy is intended to help students narrow down their ideas and write an effective topic sentence that clearly contributes to the controlling theme of the entire piece of writing.

1. Provide students with a copy of the 3-2-1 form (Figure 4.1.1).
2. Explain that well-developed topic sentences are critical to good writing. First, though, students have to identify a topic they want to write about. Next, have them write three ideas they have about the topic. Have students write these in the "3" section of the form. At this point, they can write anything they know about the topic.
3. Then have students write two details or examples pertaining to the same topic. Instruct students to write these in the "2" section of the form. The purpose of this step is for students to elaborate on their ideas.
4. The last step is for students to reread the three ideas and two details to develop a single topic sentence, which will state the main idea for the paragraph. Using students' examples, model how to write a strong topic sentence. To determine the quality of the topic sentence, answer the questions on the 3-2-1 form. These include
   • Does the topic sentence state the main point?
   • Does the topic sentence reflect the three ideas and two details?
   • Does the topic sentence invite the reader because it is interesting, exciting, or intriguing?
   • Does the topic sentence address the topic without being too narrow, broad, or vague?

If students answer "no" to these questions, they will need additional modeling, practice, and feedback.

 Tip

Consider alternating the process from 3-2-1 to 1-2-3. Some students may prefer to select a topic and develop a topic sentence first and then write their ideas, details, and examples.

Alternatives and Accommodations

- For students who are learning to speak and write in English, a key support for this strategy is to select topics with which they are familiar. The better you know your students, the easier it will be to find topics that they know something about. When they have a familiar topic, they should be able to generate ideas and details. For example, use topics that relate to their parents' occupations, where they used to live, the geography of their homeland, their families, or their favorite hobbies and activities. It is important to help students make connections to and build on their existing experiences.

- One simple way to accommodate struggling readers as they begin to use this strategy is to ask them to provide their ideas orally. You can record students' ideas as they tell them aloud and then prompt them for details, which you can also record. Finally, help students write a good topic sentence by showing them that certain key words need to be included. After recording and helping students the first few times they use this strategy, turn the process over to them. Be available for assistance, but gradually raise your expectations for independent work.

- Some of your students may have no problem thinking of ideas about a topic, but they may have difficulty generating details and then writing a topic sentence. Topic sentences seem to be a challenge for many students. To help them, model specific steps and demonstrate how to move from ideas to details to topic sentence. After modeling several examples, let students try on their own, but make yourself their editor. Edit their topic sentences and show them how to revise and improve as they write. Check their revisions and give them lots of practice so their topic sentences are clear, concise, and specific to the topic.

FIGURE 4.1.1 : 3-2-1

My topic:

_____

_____

Write **3** ideas you already know about the topic:

_____

_____

_____

_____

Write **2** details or examples about the topic:

_____

_____

_____

Reread what you wrote above. Then write **1** topic sentence that pulls it all together:

_____

_____

_____

_____

Refer to the topic sentence, and answer the questions below. If you answer "no" to these questions, edit your topic sentence.

	Yes	No
Does the topic sentence state the main point?	☐	☐
Does the topic sentence reflect the three ideas and two details?	☐	☐
Does the topic sentence invite the reader because it is interesting, exciting, or intriguing?	☐	☐
Does the topic sentence address the topic without being too narrow, broad, or vague?	☐	☐

Strategy 2: Check Yourself

Most people who write for a living have editors. The editor's job is to improve the author's writing by deleting, revising, adding, polishing, and helping him or her focus on information that is critical to the purpose. Unfortunately, most student writers do not have editors and must learn to edit themselves. This is difficult to do at first, so it is important to model the process for students and provide them with helpful tools. One tool that reminds and prompts students to check their writing against desired standards is the Check Yourself card. Learning to "check themselves" will help students improve their writing by focusing on editing out irrelevant information.

1. Give each student a copy of the Check Yourself cards (Figure 4.2.1).
2. Read the directives and questions aloud, and project a writing example for all students to read. Follow the five steps on the card, modeling the process through think-alouds.
3. Ask students to edit their own writing using the Check Yourself card as a guide.
4. After students have finished editing, ask volunteers to present their work, giving a before and after review of their writing.

 ## Tip

If students are comfortable with one another and not threatened or embarrassed by group work, you can begin with peer editing first. Students can share their suggestions, criticisms, and ideas for editing and refining one another's writing.

 ## Alternatives and Accommodations

- Begin the editing process by making sure that students have correctly used all words and phrases in the passage. If necessary, model how to check various resources for correct meanings, or suggest more specific or appropriate words students could use.
- Make sure students with reading difficulties do not get held up by the very tool that is supposed to help them. If students cannot read or understand the Check Yourself cards, then simplify them—perhaps using icons to represent each step or using fewer words.
- Some students have trouble editing because they cannot identify the main idea of their writing. Before beginning to self-edit, ask these students to set aside their writing and tell you the main idea in their own words. If they

cannot do this without reading or referring to the passage, then they may not yet know what they are writing about. Help them identify and clarify the main idea before they begin editing.

FIGURE 4.2.1 : **Check Yourself Card**

1. Read the title of your paragraph or essay.

2. Underline or highlight the topic sentence(s). Restate the main idea to yourself.

3. Read each sentence, one at a time. Ask yourself the following questions:

   - Does this sentence have something to do with the main idea?
        YES   NO

   - Does this sentence add interesting, important, or essential information?
        YES   NO

   - If I delete this sentence, will it affect the reader's understanding of the main idea? (If you are unsure, try reading the paragraph without the sentence. See if you miss it.)
        YES   NO

4. Draw a line through the sentences you think are irrelevant. Reread your paragraph and see if you think it is more focused.

---

1. Read the title of your paragraph or essay.

2. Underline or highlight the topic sentence(s). Restate the main idea to yourself.

3. Read each sentence, one at a time. Ask yourself the following questions:

   - Does this sentence have something to do with the main idea?
        YES   NO

   - Does this sentence add interesting, important, or essential information?
        YES   NO

   - If I delete this sentence, will it affect the reader's understanding of the main idea? (If you are unsure, try reading the paragraph without the sentence. See if you miss it.)
        YES   NO

4. Draw a line through the sentences you think are irrelevant. Reread your paragraph and see if you think it is more focused.

Strategy 3: Color Coding for Consistency

When writing a coherent paragraph, it is important for students to group related sentences and maintain a consistent point of view. In this activity, all students should write about the same topic. However, not all pairs will be writing from the same point of view (i.e., first person, second person, third person).

1. Assign each student a partner so they are working in pairs. After you have assigned the partners, give each pair a stack of sticky notes in one of three colors. One color (e.g., yellow) represents first person. The second color (e.g., pink) represents second person, and the third color (e.g., green) represents third person.

2. Review the pronouns associated with each point of view. First-person pronouns include *I*, *me*, *my*, *we*, *us*, *our*, and so on. Second-person pronouns include *you* and *your*. Third-person pronouns are the most numerous and include *he*, *she*, *it*, *him*, *her*, *his*, *its*, and various nouns.

3. Ask students to write one pronoun on each of their sticky notes. Point out to students that they can repeat pronouns on additional sticky notes. For example, if they want to use the word *I* five times, they will need to write it five times on five separate sticky notes. When they are finished, they should have a set of sticky notes that is one color and in the same voice.

4. Provide pairs with a writing prompt and ask them to write one sentence about it on each sticky note, including the appropriate pronoun in the sentence. They should repeat this step until they have written a five-sentence paragraph.

5. Ask students to arrange their sticky notes so their paragraphs make sense. After everyone has completed the activity (i.e., they have written their paragraphs), ask them to share their work so all students can hear examples of writing from first-person, second-person, and third-person points of view.

 Tip

Be sure to explain to students that just because they are writing from a specific point of view, there may still by other pronouns and nouns in their paragraphs. Remind students that the key is to tell a story or share information from the same perspective and refrain from writing from multiple points of view.

Alternatives and Accommodations

- Some students may need to review what *point of view* and *voice* mean and how to identify them in a piece of writing. Refer to the Three Tab POV strategy (Strategy 25) in your instruction, or use it as a prior practice activity.

- For struggling readers, the key to success here may be repetition and peer editing. If you use the strategy once and find that some students are still struggling, go back and review the pronouns for each point of view, provide more practice samples, and set students up with partners who can help them.

- Younger or less-competent writers may need to practice writing from or recognizing one point of view at a time. When this is the case, give everyone the same color sticky notes. This will allow you to focus your instruction on each point of view in turn. It will also allow students to practice using one point of view at a time and hopefully minimize confusion. After students have mastered that point of view, they can move to another.

Strategy 4: Editing Irrelevant Information

Students often have a hard time discerning relevant from irrelevant information in their writing. Consequently, they find it difficult to find and delete irrelevant information. Here are six tips and a checklist they can use to eliminate irrelevant information from their writing.

1. Project Figure 4.4.1 for the class to see.
2. Read the tips and examples aloud, and explain why deleting irrelevant information makes a sentence or paragraph clearer.
3. After the discussion, tell students to edit the paragraph on owls using the checklist.
4. Have students use the Checklist for Editing Irrelevant Information (Figure 4.4.2) to delete irrelevant information from their own work. Assign peer editors to work on this activity together.

 ## Tip

Because some students may need additional practice, prepare additional passages that contain irrelevant information. It's a good idea to have several passages ready for editing.

 ## Alternatives and Accommodations

- Editing something written in a language that is not your first can be a challenge. When using this strategy with English language learners, you may need to take one step at a time. For example, focus first on deleting unnecessary words. Repeat the activity with several different writing samples. Allow students to peer-edit one another's work. After students gain proficiency with this step, move on to the next, deleting words that repeat a concept or idea, and so on.

- For students who have difficulty reading, the key to making this strategy work is to present sentences that are at their reading level. If the readability doesn't match their level, they will not comprehend the sentences, and editing may turn into a guessing game. Before you begin, make sure you have appropriate sentences and paragraphs for reading levels of your students.

- Consider presenting students with one sentence at a time for editing. Sometimes, when students see an entire page of sentences or a long paragraph, they become overwhelmed. They may refuse to begin because they don't think they'll ever be able to finish. Use sentence strips or ask students to edit on the board, one sentence at a time.

FIGURE 4.4.1 : Six Tips for Editing Irrelevant Information

Relevant information is important to your writing; it is information critical to a reader's understanding. Irrelevant information is not important or completely unrelated. It only serves to confuse and distract the reader. Here are six tips to help you delete irrelevant information from your writing:

1. Delete unnecessary words.

You often need only one word for exaggerations.

Original: Haley is going to be a doctor because she is <u>so incredibly</u> smart.

Edited: Haley is going to be a doctor because she is smart.

Edited: Haley is going to be a doctor because she is <u>so</u> smart.

Edited: Haley is going to be a doctor because she is <u>incredibly</u> smart.

Original: I was <u>very, very, very</u> hungry.

Edited: I was <u>very</u> hungry.

Original: Mr. Alpert is <u>really, really, I mean really</u> tall.

Edited: Mr. Alpert is <u>really</u> tall.

You do not have to explain an understood concept.

Original: Saleem wants <u>to eat</u> cupcakes on his birthday.

Edited: Saleem wants cupcakes on his birthday.

(It is understood that he will eat the cupcakes.)

Original: Henry and Rosa love to <u>go out to</u> eat at that Mexican restaurant.

Edited: Henry and Rosa love to eat at that Mexican restaurant.

(It is understood that they go out to eat at a restaurant.)

Original: Adela told her friends to <u>dress up fancy</u>.

Edited: Adela told her friends to dress up.

Edited: Adela told her friends to dress fancy.

(It is understood that by dressing up, they will look fancy.)

2. Delete extra words that repeat a single concept.

Original: The baby fell and as he was falling he reached for my hand.

Edited: As the baby fell, he reached for my hand.

FIGURE 4.4.1 : Six Tips for Editing Irrelevant Information (*continued*)

Original: My dad gave my mom such beautiful, pretty flowers that looked so nice.

Edited: My dad gave my mom beautiful flowers.

Original: He has the habit of always doing that.

Edited: He has the habit of doing that.

3. Delete phrases such as *everyone says/knows that . . . , they say that . . . , and I once heard that . . .*

Original: <u>They say that</u> winters are cold in Chicago.

Edited: Winters are cold in Chicago.

Original: <u>I once heard that</u> it is better to give than to receive.

Edited: It is better to give than to receive.

Original: <u>Everyone says that</u> we should exercise and eat healthy.

Edited: We should exercise and eat healthy.

4. Delete sentences that do not relate to the topic sentence.

The underlined sentences below can be deleted, since they do not relate to the topic of the paragraph.

My friend Jose Miguel enjoys Disney World because of the rides. <u>He plans to take his friends this year</u>. His favorite ride is Space Mountain. He gets a thrill from it because it is fast. He also likes Splash Mountain because he likes to get wet. He doesn't like the Haunted Mansion because it's a slow ride.

Delores loves to bake. In fact, the pastries she bakes make her family very happy. <u>I hate to bake because I hate cleaning up the mess</u>. Her brothers like the cakes. Her parents prefer the cookies. Her grandparents can't get enough of her pies.

Kevin wants to be a dancer when he grows up. He likes the challenge of moving his body to the beat. He says he feels like he's flying when he dances. He also gets a great feeling when the audience cheers him on. His goal is to be a dancer for a famous pop star. <u>Kevin's sister is a great dancer, too.</u>

5. Combine sentences when the meaning can stay the same.

Original: Jorge lives next door to his grandmother. She's 71 years old.

Edited: Jorge lives next door to his 71-year-old grandmother.

Original: Elsa and her sister went shopping at the mall. They were looking for prom dresses.

Edited: Elsa and her sister went shopping for prom dresses.

Original: President Obama was in New York. He was attending a reception at the United Nations.

Edited: President Obama was in New York attending a reception at the United Nations.

6. Change passive voice to active voice whenever possible.

Sentences written in the passive voice often include unnecessary words. An active voice can also make the meaning of the sentence clearer.

Original: The driveway was stained by the truck.

Edited: The truck stained the driveway.

Original: The following facts must be included in your essay for it to get a passing grade.

Edited: Include the following facts in your essay for a passing grade.

Original: The permission form has to be signed by your parents.

Edited: Your parents have to sign the permission form.

Now it's your turn. Use the six steps to delete irrelevant information from the following paragraph.

The owls in this region of the country are night hunters. I've seen them fly over my house. At night, they go hunting for food. We all know they hunt small animals such as mice, rabbits, and squirrels. Some groundhogs have even been caught by them. They have great and excellent vision, which makes it super easy for them to catch their prey they are hunting. They also have great hearing which helps them hear rodents scurrying hundreds of feet away in the distance.

FIGURE 4.4.2 : Checklist for Editing Irrelevant Information

Name: _____ Date: _____

Essay Title: _____

My Checklist for Editing Irrelevant Information	Yes	No	N/A
I deleted unnecessary words.	☐	☐	☐
I deleted extra words that repeated a single concept.	☐	☐	☐
I deleted phrases such as *everyone says/knows that . . ., they say that . . . , and I once heard that . . .*	☐	☐	☐
I deleted sentences that did not relate to the topic sentence.	☐	☐	☐
I combined sentences when the meaning could stay the same.	☐	☐	☐
I changed passive voice to active voice whenever possible.	☐	☐	☐

Peer Editor's Checklist for Editing Irrelevant Information	Yes	No	N/A
My peer deleted unnecessary words.	☐	☐	☐
My peer deleted extra words that repeated a single concept.	☐	☐	☐
My peer deleted phrases such as *everyone says/knows that . . ., they say that . . . , and I once heard that . . .*	☐	☐	☐
My peer deleted sentences that did not relate to the topic sentence.	☐	☐	☐
My peer combined sentences when the meaning could stay the same.	☐	☐	☐
My peer changed passive voice to active voice whenever possible.	☐	☐	☐

Teacher's Checklist for Editing Irrelevant Information	Yes	No	N/A
The student deleted unnecessary words.	☐	☐	☐
The student deleted extra words that repeated a single concept.	☐	☐	☐
The student deleted phrases such as *everyone says/knows that . . ., they say that . . . , and I once heard that . . .*	☐	☐	☐
The student deleted sentences that did not relate to the topic sentence.	☐	☐	☐
The student combined sentences when the meaning could stay the same.	☐	☐	☐
The student changed passive voice to active voice whenever possible.	☐	☐	☐

Strategy 5: Figurative Language Cards

Figurative language can engage readers by evoking their emotions and feelings through descriptive words and statements. Figurative language includes alliteration, assonance, onomatopoeia, simile, metaphor, hyperbole, personification, irony, idioms, and rhetorical language. Figurative language can make writing come alive. However, many struggling writers have a difficult time using figurative language in their work because there are an infinite number of ways to incorporate it into writing, and the choices tend to overwhelm them. To help students get into the practice of using figurative language more naturally and consistently, consider leading them through some activities with the figurative language cards we've included here (Figures 4.5.1 through 4.5.10).

1. Teach students about the purpose of figurative language and the specific examples of alliteration, assonance, onomatopoeia, simile, metaphor, hyperbole, personification, irony, idioms, and rhetorical language. Explain that they will be playing a card game that reinforces these concepts.

2. Depending on their existing understanding of these concepts, students can play with two sets of figurative language cards (e.g., similes and metaphors), three sets (e.g., onomatopoeia, alliteration, and assonance), five sets (e.g., hyperbole, personification, irony, idiom, and rhetorical language), or as many as you deem appropriate.

3. Make copies of the cards you want to use. The concept term and definition should be on one side, and the relevant example statement should appear on the other.

4. Divide students into pairs, give each pair a set of cards, and have them cut out the cards.

5. Have students shuffle the cards so the example statements are face up and the respective terms and definitions are face down. Students should take turns choosing a card, reading the statement aloud, and then classifying the statement by identifying which type of the figurative language it represents. (For example, if Victoria chooses a card and reads, "My cat's eyes are as blue as the sea," she could respond by saying, "It's a simile because a comparison is made using the word *as*." She would then turn the card over to confirm her decision.) Consider making blank cards available so your students can brainstorm their own examples and extend the activity.

6. As an extension, provide pairs of students with a short story, novel, newspaper or magazine article, or a selection of grade-level content from a social studies or science textbook. Have students alternate choosing a card and

looking for examples of that type of figurative language in the passage. If there are no instances of figurative language in the passage, challenge students to identify a logical place where they might insert a relevant example.

7. Once students are comfortable with identifying figurative language, encourage them to look for statements in their own writing that can be enhanced with descriptive, figurative language.

8. To further reinforce effective use of figurative language, have students pick a card and then show them a picture of a familiar food or household product. They should then write an advertisement or other piece of persuasive writing using a relevant example of figurative language.

 Tip

After the activity, shuffle the figurative language cards and ask each student to choose three. Students can then write a paragraph, essay, or composition that includes all three devices.

 Alternatives and Accommodations

- Understanding and using figurative language can be especially challenging for students whose first language is not English. Figurative language not only doesn't correspond to literal definitions of words but also has the hidden meanings that are usually difficult to explain. For English language learners, consider using only one type of figurative language card at a time. Ask students to read the cards and explain what they mean. If they understand the meanings, discuss why the example fits a specific category of figurative language. Later, students can review each type with additional sets of cards.

- For students who need to review examples of figurative language, assign them the task of making their own personal set of cards. This will allow them to study during downtime in the classroom and while at home. Several websites and mobile apps allow students to create their own flashcards and download them to smartphones, tablets, or other mobile devices. Students can also quiz themselves with self-created tests.

- Some students will be uncomfortable joining in a group game. For these students, assign partners and let them work in pairs first. After they relax and are less self-conscious, move to groups of three or four students and monitor each group for social skills such as turn-taking, complimenting and encouraging others, staying with the group, and completing the assignment.

FIGURE 4.5.1 : Alliteration Cards

Alliteration

consonant sounds that are repeated
at the beginning of words

- sounds like a tongue twister
- used to emphasize certain words

Alliteration

consonant sounds that are repeated
at the beginning of words

- sounds like a tongue twister
- used to emphasize certain words

Alliteration

consonant sounds that are repeated
at the beginning of words

- sounds like a tongue twister
- used to emphasize certain words

Alliteration

consonant sounds that are repeated
at the beginning of words

- sounds like a tongue twister
- used to emphasize certain words

Alliteration

consonant sounds that are repeated
at the beginning of words

- sounds like a tongue twister
- used to emphasize certain words

Alliteration

consonant sounds that are repeated
at the beginning of words

- sounds like a tongue twister
- used to emphasize certain words

Alliteration

consonant sounds that are repeated
at the beginning of words

- sounds like a tongue twister
- used to emphasize certain words

Alliteration

consonant sounds that are repeated
at the beginning of words

- sounds like a tongue twister
- used to emphasize certain words

Alliteration

consonant sounds that are repeated
at the beginning of words

- sounds like a tongue twister
- used to emphasize certain words

Alliteration

consonant sounds that are repeated
at the beginning of words

- sounds like a tongue twister
- used to emphasize certain words

FIGURE 4.5.1 : Alliteration Cards (*continued*)

Peter Piper picked a peck of pickled peppers.

Alex's aunts Amy and Ashley always answer their phone.

Simon sang his song sweet and softly.

Frank's favorite fast food is pizza.

Carlos can count his coins while caressing his cat.

Thurston Thames thanked his father on Thursday.

Wanda was wary of Wendy's ways.

Chandler chooses to champion for Chester.

Larry loses lots of lollipops.

Gary got greedy and grubby.

FIGURE 4.5.2 : Assonance Cards

Assonance vowel sounds that are repeated • generally used to create a specific mood	**Assonance** vowel sounds that are repeated • generally used to create a specific mood
Assonance vowel sounds that are repeated • generally used to create a specific mood	**Assonance** vowel sounds that are repeated • generally used to create a specific mood
Assonance vowel sounds that are repeated • generally used to create a specific mood	**Assonance** vowel sounds that are repeated • generally used to create a specific mood
Assonance vowel sounds that are repeated • generally used to create a specific mood	**Assonance** vowel sounds that are repeated • generally used to create a specific mood
Assonance vowel sounds that are repeated • generally used to create a specific mood	**Assonance** vowel sounds that are repeated • generally used to create a specific mood

FIGURE 4.5.2 : Assonance Cards (*continued*)

She eerily erased Yvonne from the email list.	Ben effortlessly texted Ted.
Pat sat admiring the slab of ham.	Ophelia owns toy boats that float.
I'm inspired to hire that retiree.	Jim's pig sips its water.
The annoyed employer avoided eye contact.	Don refused to eat what he believed was a rotted hot dog.
Olivia only bought oily olives.	Aging aliens ate acres of tomatoes.

FIGURE 4.5.3 : Onomatopoeia Cards

Onomatopoeia

words that mimic the sound they represent

- syllables sound like a real sound
  - appeals to the senses

Onomatopoeia

words that mimic the sound they represent

- syllables sound like a real sound
  - appeals to the senses

Onomatopoeia

words that mimic the sound they represent

- syllables sound like a real sound
  - appeals to the senses

Onomatopoeia

words that mimic the sound they represent

- syllables sound like a real sound
  - appeals to the senses

Onomatopoeia

words that mimic the sound they represent

- syllables sound like a real sound
  - appeals to the senses

Onomatopoeia

words that mimic the sound they represent

- syllables sound like a real sound
  - appeals to the senses

Onomatopoeia

words that mimic the sound they represent

- syllables sound like a real sound
  - appeals to the senses

Onomatopoeia

words that mimic the sound they represent

- syllables sound like a real sound
  - appeals to the senses

Onomatopoeia

words that mimic the sound they represent

- syllables sound like a real sound
  - appeals to the senses

Onomatopoeia

words that mimic the sound they represent

- syllables sound like a real sound
  - appeals to the senses

FIGURE 4.5.3 : Onomatopoeia Cards (continued)

All night long, I hear, "Drip . . . drip . . . drip."	"Poof!" And the rabbit appeared.
You could hear the murmur of the bugs.	The car came to a screeching halt.
We were startled when we heard, "ding dong."	The cow mooed when she saw me.
The player was down at the first "pow!"	The fly's buzzing was driving me crazy.
"Hmmm. I wonder when she's coming."	"Rrrrrrr," snarled the dog.

FIGURE 4.5.4 : Simile Cards

Simile	Simile
a comparison of two different things using the word *like* or *as*	a comparison of two different things using the word *like* or *as*
Simile	Simile
a comparison of two different things using the word *like* or *as*	a comparison of two different things using the word *like* or *as*
Simile	Simile
a comparison of two different things using the word *like* or *as*	a comparison of two different things using the word *like* or *as*
Simile	Simile
a comparison of two different things using the word *like* or *as*	a comparison of two different things using the word *like* or *as*
Simile	Simile
a comparison of two different things using the word *like* or *as*	a comparison of two different things using the word *like* or *as*

FIGURE 4.5.4 : Simile Cards (*continued*)

Sarah is as tall as a telephone pole.	My cat's eyes are as blue as the sea.
Jasper wrestles like a bull.	Paul is as slender as a ferret.
That bed is like a torture rack.	Ali's shoes are like canoes.
The diamond sparkled like a star.	They are as loud as hyenas.
The floors were as shiny as a mirror.	Her hair glistened like the sun.

FIGURE 4.5.5 : **Metaphor Cards**

Metaphor a comparison of two different things using a form of the verb *be*	**Metaphor** a comparison of two different things using a form of the verb *be*
Metaphor a comparison of two different things using a form of the verb *be*	**Metaphor** a comparison of two different things using a form of the verb *be*
Metaphor a comparison of two different things using a form of the verb *be*	**Metaphor** a comparison of two different things using a form of the verb *be*
Metaphor a comparison of two different things using a form of the verb *be*	**Metaphor** a comparison of two different things using a form of the verb *be*
Metaphor a comparison of two different things using a form of the verb *be*	**Metaphor** a comparison of two different things using a form of the verb *be*

FIGURE 4.5.5 : Metaphor Cards (*continued*)

That 3-year-old is a jumping kangaroo. He never stays put.

These glasses are my eyes.

Rajesh has the memory of an elephant.

Joel is a camel and can go without drinking water for an entire day.

Janice is the sunshine of my day.

Ali's shoes are canoes.

Carlos is a walking computer.

Mr. Cuellar is a dinosaur.

That car is a tank.

My grandfather is a wise owl.

FIGURE 4.5.6 : Hyperbole Cards

Hyperbole an exaggeration used to emphasize a point • not taken literally	**Hyperbole** an exaggeration used to emphasize a point • not taken literally
Hyperbole an exaggeration used to emphasize a point • not taken literally	**Hyperbole** an exaggeration used to emphasize a point • not taken literally
Hyperbole an exaggeration used to emphasize a point • not taken literally	**Hyperbole** an exaggeration used to emphasize a point • not taken literally
Hyperbole an exaggeration used to emphasize a point • not taken literally	**Hyperbole** an exaggeration used to emphasize a point • not taken literally
Hyperbole an exaggeration used to emphasize a point • not taken literally	**Hyperbole** an exaggeration used to emphasize a point • not taken literally

FIGURE 4.5.6 : Hyperbole Cards (*continued*)

He is the best dancer in the whole wide world.	Pablo has the skills of a surgeon.
Those gym shoes kill me every time.	Irene has money to burn.
That kid is a genius.	That was the most delicious steak ever.
Lupe has the voice of an angel.	Rosario is a real saint for putting up with her neighbor.
He is as skinny as a toothpick.	She eats like a bird.

FIGURE 4.5.7 : Personification Cards

Personification

when an inanimate object is given
human or animal qualities

- used to make an object more relatable
- gives a sense of personality to something that normally
wouldn't have one

Personification

when an inanimate object is given
human or animal qualities

- used to make an object more relatable
- gives a sense of personality to something that normally
wouldn't have one

Personification

when an inanimate object is given
human or animal qualities

- used to make an object more relatable
- gives a sense of personality to something that normally
wouldn't have one

Personification

when an inanimate object is given
human or animal qualities

- used to make an object more relatable
- gives a sense of personality to something that normally
wouldn't have one

Personification

when an inanimate object is given
human or animal qualities

- used to make an object more relatable
- gives a sense of personality to something that normally
wouldn't have one

Personification

when an inanimate object is given
human or animal qualities

- used to make an object more relatable
- gives a sense of personality to something that normally
wouldn't have one

Personification

when an inanimate object is given
human or animal qualities

- used to make an object more relatable
- gives a sense of personality to something that normally
wouldn't have one

Personification

when an inanimate object is given
human or animal qualities

- used to make an object more relatable
- gives a sense of personality to something that normally
wouldn't have one

Personification

when an inanimate object is given
human or animal qualities

- used to make an object more relatable
- gives a sense of personality to something that normally
wouldn't have one

Personification

when an inanimate object is given
human or animal qualities

- used to make an object more relatable
- gives a sense of personality to something that normally
wouldn't have one

FIGURE 4.5.7 : Personification Cards (*continued*)

The pen danced all over that page.	The book was screaming, "Read me!"
The desk knew it could no longer take the weight.	That front door turned everyone away.
Those French fries are calling my name.	Their backyard is starving for some attention.
Her house is crying for a new roof.	My bed knew I wanted to nap.
My car hates me.	The walls in this house have ears.

FIGURE 4.5.8 : Irony Cards

Irony when the meaning of a statement is the exact opposite of what the words suggest	**Irony** when the meaning of a statement is the exact opposite of what the words suggest
Irony when the meaning of a statement is the exact opposite of what the words suggest	**Irony** when the meaning of a statement is the exact opposite of what the words suggest
Irony when the meaning of a statement is the exact opposite of what the words suggest	**Irony** when the meaning of a statement is the exact opposite of what the words suggest
Irony when the meaning of a statement is the exact opposite of what the words suggest	**Irony** when the meaning of a statement is the exact opposite of what the words suggest
Irony when the meaning of a statement is the exact opposite of what the words suggest	**Irony** when the meaning of a statement is the exact opposite of what the words suggest

FIGURE 4.5.8 : **Irony Cards** (*continued*)

Everyone hates the bonus we just got.	That's all I need—more trouble.
It looks like you are begging for more homework.	Oh joy! Another bill to pay.
Let me just take a million dollars out of my wallet and lend it to you.	I know you don't want to go to Disneyland because of all the walking you would do.
We all love to pay taxes.	I'm so busy I'd have to turn down a restful vacation.
My speedy sports car stalled.	I just want you to rest during PE.

FIGURE 4.5.9 : Idiom Cards

Idiom a conventional expression	**Idiom** a conventional expression
Idiom a conventional expression	**Idiom** a conventional expression
Idiom a conventional expression	**Idiom** a conventional expression
Idiom a conventional expression	**Idiom** a conventional expression
Idiom a conventional expression	**Idiom** a conventional expression

FIGURE 4.5.9 : Idiom Cards (*continued*)

Let's catch some rays.	For what it's worth, they plan to reassign you to another classroom.
He's a pain in the neck.	It's down to the wire and we still don't know who'll be eliminated from the game.
Will you soften up?	It's his fancy footwork that gets him into trouble.
I'm going around in circles trying to explain this.	Let's wipe the slate clean and rework our math problem.
Her speech was a breath of fresh air.	As she dove into the pool, she said, "Here goes nothing."

FIGURE 4.5.10 : **Rhetorical Cards**

Rhetorical Language

an assertion posed as a question

- question isn't really meant to be answered

Rhetorical Language

an assertion posed as a question

- question isn't really meant to be answered

Rhetorical Language

an assertion posed as a question

question isn't really meant to be answered

Rhetorical Language

an assertion posed as a question

- question isn't really meant to be answered

Rhetorical Language

an assertion posed as a question

- question isn't really meant to be answered

Rhetorical Language

an assertion posed as a question

- question isn't really meant to be answered

Rhetorical Language

an assertion posed as a question

- question isn't really meant to be answered

Rhetorical Language

an assertion posed as a question

- question isn't really meant to be answered

Rhetorical Language

an assertion posed as a question

- question isn't really meant to be answered

Rhetorical Language

an assertion posed as a question

- question isn't really meant to be answered

FIGURE 4.5.10 : Rhetorical Cards (continued)

How many times must I tell you to clean your room?	Is it hot/cold enough for you?
Who would have known that it was going to be a mild winter?	What will Ms. Nelson think of next?
They expect us to believe that?	Could you be any smarter?
Who could have predicted he would win the presidency?	What part of "no" don't you understand?
Who knows?	Can I have your attention, please?

Strategy 6: Flying High

When writing compositions, students need to know not only how to write a coherent paragraph but also how to combine several ideas into separate, but related, paragraphs. One way to help students learn this skill is to practice using a graphic organizer. Students can use our Flying High organizer to help them connect one paragraph to the next. In addition, this strategy is a useful prewriting tool that allows students to collect and arrange their thoughts before they begin writing. In short, they can complete the graphic organizer to recognize the links between and among ideas in each paragraph and to ensure that their paragraphs lead to a logical conclusion (e.g., culminating paragraph).

1. Distribute a double-sided copy of the Flying High graphic organizer to each student (Figure 4.6.1). Point out the main frame of the kite and the smaller bows along the tailstring.
2. Have students write the topic and the important details they want to include in the opening paragraph on the frame of the kite.
3. Students should then decide on the separate ideas they want to develop in the other paragraphs, making sure they lead to a strong conclusion.
4. Encourage students to work in pairs or small groups to discuss how they plan to arrange their thoughts, along with their reasons and justifications for this arrangement. Explain to students that as peer editors, their role is to suggest ways that their peers' writing can be improved. Any negative feedback should be accompanied by a positive suggestion.
5. After listening to their peers' constructive feedback, students should write the main idea of each paragraph in the separate bows along the kite's string.
6. On the opposite side of each bow (i.e., the other side of the paper), students should write supporting details for each main idea.
7. After completing the graphic organizer, students should have a good overview of and direction for their writing. They can now begin writing their compositions with a clear focus.

 ## Tip

The Flying High organizer can also be used to teach specific concepts related to writing. For example, after learning about metaphors, students can write a topic on the kite (e.g., chocolate), and then write a series of metaphors on the bows (e.g., The brown gold broke in my hands). Likewise, to develop their vocabulary, students can write a word on the kite (e.g., *conform*), and then write a series of synonyms on the bows (e.g., *accommodate, adjust, integrate, obey,* etc.).

Alternatives and Accommodations

- Students can cut out the kite and bows and string them together. This will allow students to flip the bows with ease so they can ensure that each paragraph's main idea and details are related and that each paragraph relates to the overall topic of the composition.

- For students who have difficulty sequencing their ideas so their writing stays coherent and logical, cut out and number the bows and let students physically organize them. If something is not in the right order, they can rearrange the order of the paragraphs *before* they start writing, which should help prevent mistakes that slow them down and frustrate them. This approach is also a subtle and clever way to introduce or reinforce the importance of organized outlines.

- Some students will need to write just one paragraph at a time. For these students, use the organizer not for separate paragraphs but for one paragraph's main idea and supporting details. Later, you can expand the activity to focus on multiple paragraphs by putting two or more kites together.

FIGURE 4.6.1 : Flying High Graphic Organizer

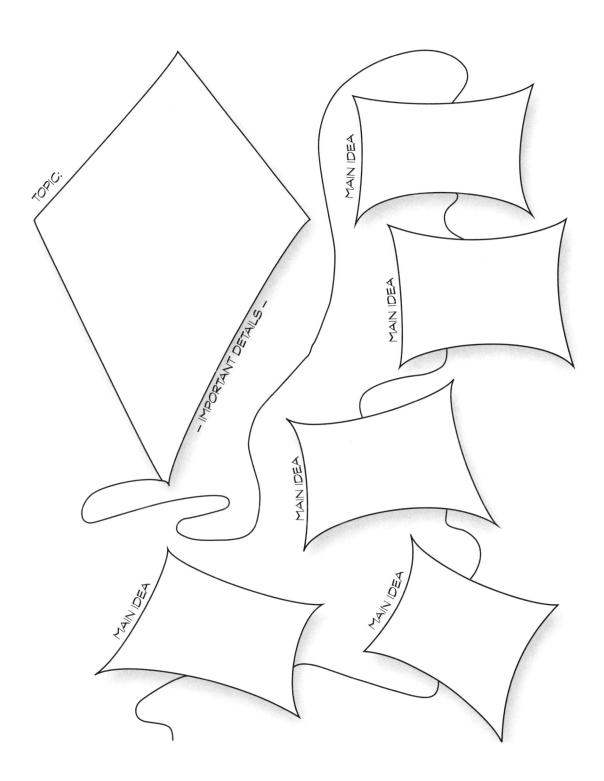

FIGURE 4.6.1 : Flying High Graphic Organizer (continued)

Strategy 7: Give Acting a Shot

One way to demonstrate the importance of the writer's voice is to have students act out a scene. Explain that, just like their performances need a unique style in order to be memorable, so do their stories and essays. That unique style is the writer's voice, which brings a topic to life and engages the audience.

1. Copy and organize the Give Acting a Shot cards (Figure 4.7.1). These cards represent various scenarios that students can act out, matching their style and voice to the intended purpose. There are two cards per letter: one scenario requires a specific voice, and the other requires a different voice. For example, the *A* cards pertain to the same situation but from two different perspectives. Therefore, each should be acted out in a different voice.

2. Call on two students, and give each a card with the same letter. Ask them to act out their scenes in front of the class. Explain that they have to use a voice that is appropriate and corresponds to the situation.

3. Encourage students to be unique and try to elicit feelings from the identified audience. Connect this activity to how good writing gives life to words and engages the reader.

4. Continue the exercise by calling on different students and having them select different cards.

5. Have students identify the main ideas and supporting details associated with each scenario. These can be written (or projected) on the board for students who need visual stimuli while brainstorming.

6. After a discussion of the ideas and details, ask students to begin writing a paragraph or essay using the displayed information. Model how voice is manifested in a central theme, main idea, and supporting details.

 Tip

Pair students and have them create their own scenarios using their own voice. Before they act out these scenarios, they can generate a list of adjectives that describe their respective voices.

 Alternatives and Accommodations

- English language learners can be paired with strong English speakers/writers for this strategy. Most of the scenarios we provided ask students to take opposite sides of a situation. If the first student is a strong English speaker and demonstrates his or her unique voice, then it is a bit easier for the other student to do the complete opposite. While they are acting out the scenarios, students should not be adversarial just because they express different voices. For example, one student may project a sad voice while the other projects a happy voice. They are not necessarily debating or arguing with each other.

- This strategy should be a good one for students who have difficulty reading. It involves a lot of action and talking, so students are not required to do a lot of higher-level reading. However, the writing step may be a challenge, so use some simple supports such as highlighting. Ask students to highlight the topic sentence in one color and then highlight specific words and phrases they use to emphasize their voice in a second color. Make sure you ask them explain how and why they chose the language they used.

- Some students may feel awkward acting out a scene in front of their peers. To help them overcome their initial discomfort, act out one or two scenarios with them. Take turns, and don't be hesitant to get dramatic. If students see that their teacher is willing to get a little silly and pretend, then they may feel more comfortable doing so themselves. Model how to project a personal voice when acting out the scenarios.

FIGURE 4.7.1 : Give Acting a Shot Cards

A.	You want to borrow your friend's video game.	A.	You don't want to lend your video game to your friend.
B.	You think Six Flags is the best place in the world.	B.	You'd rather go to Disney World than Six Flags.
C.	You want a role in a school play.	C.	You think school plays are a waste of time.
D.	Convince your mother to let you watch your favorite TV show.	D.	Explain to your mother why you would rather be out with friends than watching TV.
E.	You want hamburgers and fries for dinner.	E.	You want to eat healthy.
F.	You want to walk home from school instead of taking the bus.	F.	You want to take the bus home from school so you can socialize with your friends.
G.	You broke your friend's cell phone.	G.	You fixed your friend's broken cell phone.
H.	You want your friends to visit you on Saturday morning.	H.	You want to have some time alone on Saturday morning.
I.	You want to see a funny movie.	I.	You want to see an action movie.
J.	You can't wait for your new pair of glasses.	J.	You think wearing glasses makes you look silly.
K.	You want the same kind of sneakers that everyone else is wearing.	K.	You want a style of sneaker that is unique.
L.	You prefer fruits and vegetables for a snack.	L.	You think chocolate bars are the perfect energy booster.

Strategy 8: Graphic Organizers

Graphic organizers are excellent tools that help writers organize their thoughts and information. They help students write inviting paragraphs with strong topic sentences, smooth transitions, good pacing, and strong story elements. The graphic organizers we include here address a variety of skills related to organization and coherence.

It is important to model the steps needed to use each organizer, providing visual examples while modeling. You should also show before and after examples (i.e., a blank form and a completed form) before expecting students to use the organizers. Students need practice, guidance, and feedback on how to use the organizers correctly before they are expected to use them independently. It's important to remind students that they can and should refer back to their graphic organizers as they write their compositions.

1. **Map It Out** (Figure 4.8.1): Have each student identify a central topic, concept, or theme for his or her composition and write it in the center circle. Students can then include the supporting ideas they plan to write about in the outer ring of circles that surrounds the center.

2. **Spider Map** (Figure 4.8.2): The spider map organizer is more detailed than Map It Out and allows students to group supporting details into subheadings (e.g., a spider map can be used when writing multiple paragraphs on the same topic). Explain to students that spider maps can be used to brainstorm and organize ideas. Demonstrate that the overall topic goes in the oval at the center of the map; this is the theme the writer wants to discuss. The legs represent the separate main ideas that will support discussion of that theme. The additional lines along each leg should be used to record supporting details for that main idea. Model using the form with a familiar text, starting with the theme or topic, then the main ideas, and then the details.

3. **Picture Story Map** (Figure 4.8.3): Explain to students that this graphic organizer will help them sequence their ideas visually. They can draw or write about an important event in each of the panels. The events should be included in a logical sequential order. Beneath each of the panels, have them write sequencing words—such as *first*, *next*, *then*, and *finally*—they should use in their compositions.

4. **Timeline** (Figure 4.8.4): This organizer is a great tool to help students as they prewrite and plan biographies, autobiographies, or historical nonfiction pieces. As students decide what they want to write about, they should identify important and appropriate events and the dates on which they occurred.

These dates go in the central arrow, and the corresponding events are written in the connected boxes. Explain that, along with the important dates and events, students still need to include smooth transitions, supporting details, and interesting facts to make their writing more engaging and interesting.

 Tip

Not all graphic organizers make sense to all people. Teach students to recognize what works for them. Expose them to many different types of organizers that can be used for writing, and encourage each student to try them all and choose those that work best for him or her.

 Alternatives and Accommodations

- English language learners often have great ideas, but their relative lack of reading and language proficiency holds them back when they try to write. Some of these organizers, such as the Picture Story Map, allow students to begin with pictures instead of fully formed sentences. This helps them generate good ideas *before* they try to write, which can usually reduce the pressure they feel and help them think of interesting topics. After they have generated ideas with pictures, teachers can help them think of appropriate vocabulary and with the mechanics of the writing.

- When students are working in pairs or small groups, using graphic organizers can be an exciting and helpful way for them to work together and create their best writing on a topic. Allow students to complete prewriting graphic organizers independently, and then combine their ideas into one "master" graphic organizer. This should result in a product that includes the best efforts from each student and allows them all to feel as if they participated in the group activity.

- While most students find graphic organizers helpful, some students may have difficulty making a connection between visual representations of ideas and their own writing. For these students, take a step-by-step instructional approach. Instead of starting with an entire organizer, divide and cut the paper into smaller sections and use one section at a time. For example, with the timeline, identify the theme or main topic, and then ask students to pick one related date and event to write about. Add that information to an empty box and post it on the board. Then record another date and event, and post that box before or after the first one, as appropriate. Finally, arrange all of the information in proper sequential order and connect them all together with a unifying arrow to create a finished written product.

FIGURE 4.8.1 : Map It Out

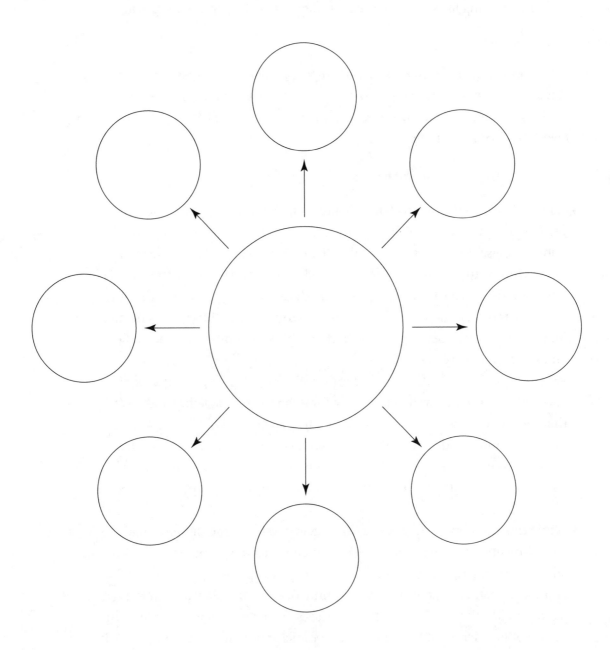

FIGURE 4.8.2 : Spider Map

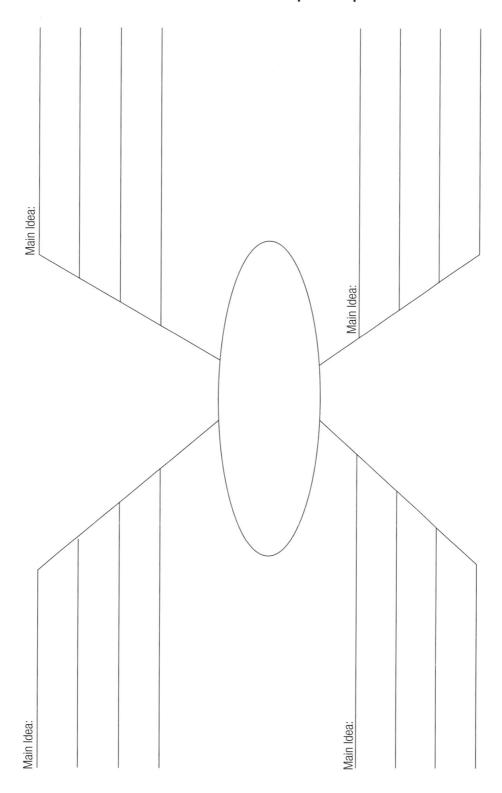

FIGURE 4.8.3 : Picture Story Map

FIGURE 4.8.4 : Timeline

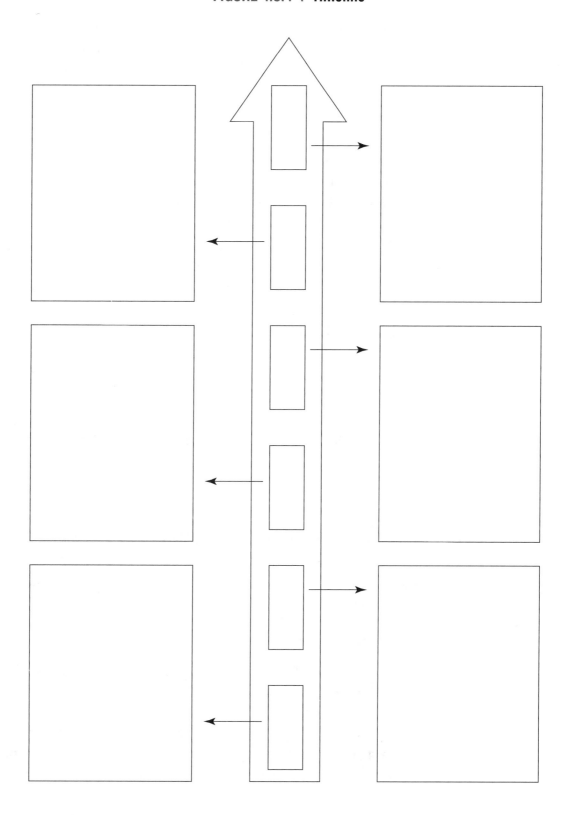

Strategy 9: Let the Senses Help

Good writers have well-developed ideas that reveal depth of thought and substance. Their writing is filled with vivid images that make their work unique and offer individual perspective. One way to help students enhance their writing is to use their senses as a guide. Words and phrases associated with their senses can be used to create strong images that connect readers to their writing.

1. Explain that high-quality writing is not only functional but also lively and passionate. Good writing is full of imagery that conveys meaning, and good writers spend time fully developing their ideas.
2. Distribute a copy of Figure 4.9.1 to each student.
3. Tell students to think about an idea they would like to develop fully. Have them write this idea at the top of the form. This idea can be a central theme of a longer work, the main point of a paragraph, or a supporting detail. An example is provided in Figure 4.9.2; feel free to share this with students as they prepare to do their own.
4. Have students make a list of words and phrases that create strong images about their idea. Beside each sense heading, they can list nouns, adverbs, adjectives, similes, metaphors, and other vibrant phrases that describe that sense.
5. After they have created the list, have them choose words and phrases that best capture the image they want to convey to readers. They can write the sentence at the bottom of the form.

Tip

This is a great opportunity to combine strategies. You may wish to use Strategy 17 (Rich Language Generator) and Strategy 29 (Vocabulary Line-Up) in conjunction with this one. Using these three strategies will give students a lot of support for expanding and enriching their vocabulary. Organize students into pairs or small groups, and have them generate a list of words and phrases.

Alternatives and Accommodations

- Usually, descriptive words and phrases that have strong connotations or implied meanings—including similes and metaphors—do not translate well from one language to another. Teaching students how to describe something in English when their own language does not have an equivalent word or phrase can be a challenge. To help English language learners succeed with this strategy, start by describing familiar people, places, and things. If necessary, provide a list of objects or people in and around school or the neighborhood. Make connections and help them build a rich language with those examples.

- For students who have difficulty reading grade-level content, provide linking words, such as *like* or *as*. For example, after students think of an adjective to describe something or someone, add a linking word and then have them finish the phrase (e.g., loud *as* a cannon). With a little help, students will create descriptive, figurative language without even realizing it!

- For students who may be more concrete thinkers and find it difficult to use imagery, take a step-by-step approach. For example, if you are asking them to describe what something sounds like, play audio recordings of various sounds and let them begin to describe each one. You can take the same approach for the other senses. Expose your students to a wide variety of experiences, and encourage them to describe those experiences, one sense at a time.

FIGURE 4.9.1 : Let the Senses Help

Your idea:

Sound:

Sight:

Smell:

Touch:

Taste:

Your well-developed idea with details:

FIGURE 4.9.2 : **Let the Senses Help Example**

Your idea:

The fox was running fast.

Sound: *quiet, like a whisper*

Sight: *red, large, fluffy, long, hurriedly, vibrant, swift*

Smell:

Touch: *soft, like a feather; wet from the morning dew*

Taste:

Your well-developed idea with details:

The red, long fox, whose fur was like a feather to touch, hurried by quietly.

Strategy 10: Listen to It

Students often write compositions that are uninteresting because they have not learned how a unique voice can make the written word more engaging. Help students better understand that the voice of a piece of writing has a unique personality that can convey feelings of humor, anger, sadness, or almost any emotion. They, as writers, have the power to elicit specific responses from their readers. Reinforce this concept by having students listen to and analyze songs they like.

1. Explain and emphasize the difference between literal and figurative language. Use the chart found in Figure 4.10.1 to emphasize the similarities and differences between literal and figurative language. Explain how writers use both to let their personalities come through their words and how a writer's voice should suit the topic, purpose, and audience of a piece of writing. Ask students to brainstorm and suggest other examples of literal and figurative language and explain how they evoke feelings in the reader.

2. Choose a popular song to play for your students. Make sure you have previewed the song so you know that the topic and language are appropriate and not offensive. Ensure that the lyrics include examples of the songwriter's or singer's voice.

3. Listen to the song once, and then play it again while students complete the Listen to It form (Parts I–III) (Figure 4.10.2). Emphasize how the artist was honest, used various expressions, and tried to connect with the listener.

4. Explain that you and the students will alter the original song from its current voice to another. To do this, refer to Part IV of Figure 4.10.2 and identify the feelings, emotions, and voice of the song in its current form. Ask students for examples of figurative language that evokes those feelings and voice.

5. Choose a new voice for the song, and check one of the boxes on the form to indicate that new voice (Part IV). Ask students to suggest similar lyrics but write them in the new voice.

6. Finally, ask students to choose a favorite song and repeat the activity with that song. Encourage students to share the original and rewritten songs with the class, and encourage the whole group to identify examples of literal and figurative language and how the voice changed between the two versions. This activity is an effective approach to teaching students how changes in language can change the tone, feelings, and voice of a composition.

Tip

Songs with subtle or equivocal lyrics can make it difficult for students to recognize voice. If students are having difficulty, select a song that is written in a strong voice. This will make it easier for students to identify the voice and recognize examples of figurative language.

 Alternatives and Accommodations

- This activity is a great opportunity to include other languages by encouraging students who speak languages other than English to share songs in their native languages and then explain to the class what the literal and figurative meanings of the words and phrases are.

- Some students may be more successful at drawing what they feel than they are at putting their feelings into words. The goal is obviously for them to write, but as a warm-up activity, have students draw pictures of how the song makes them feel. They can then label their pictures with adjectives and other descriptive terms.

- This activity might be embarrassing for students who are not comfortable sharing their feelings in public. In order to encourage all students to participate, allow volunteers to share their revised compositions instead of singling out students and calling on them to present. Students who aren't comfortable speaking in front of the class can explain their feelings when they write. Allowing partners to work together is also helpful for this activity.

FIGURE 4.10.1 : Examples of Literal and Figurative Language

Literal Language actual or close description of the meaning of the word(s)	Figurative Language a figure of speech (such as a metaphor); language that is not literal
Her grandmother *died*.	Her grandmother *is at rest*.
My brother *eats a lot*.	My brother eats *like a hungry goat*.
I've got to lose this *weight*.	I've got to lose this *tire around my waist*.
Miranda called to complain about *her boss*.	Miranda called to complain about *the banshee*.
He *made a lot of money*.	He *really hit paydirt*.
That laptop *is old*.	*Cavemen used* that laptop.
Her hair could *use some conditioner*.	Her hair *is a horse's mane*.
It's going to be *hot and humid* tomorrow.	It's going to be a *steam bath* tomorrow.
That is a *very uncomfortable* mattress.	That mattress is a *torture rack*.
Her mom *has a long list of chores for her to do*.	Her mom *works her to death*.
The prom dress was *expensive*.	I spent *an arm and a leg* on that prom dress.

FIGURE 4.10.2 : **Listen To It**

Every artist has a unique voice with a heart and soul that comes through in his or her music. Listen closely to the lyrics of your favorite song, and answer the following questions to help you think about your own unique voice.

I.   Information about the song:

Title of the song: _____

Singer/Songwriter: _____

Topic of the song: _____

II.   Your feelings associated with the song:

What are some feelings you get as you listen to the song?

_____

_____

_____

_____

What are some words that give you this feeling?

_____

_____

_____

_____

III.   Identify examples of literal and figurative language in the song. What are some ways to change literal language to figurative language and vice versa?

Literal language	Figurative language

(continued)

FIGURE 4.10.2 : Listen To It (continued)

IV.   Think about a fresh take on the song. How can you change the voice of the song to your own with a unique set of feelings and emotions?

Original version:	New version:
☐ Humorous	☐ Humorous
☐ Angry	☐ Angry
☐ Sad	☐ Sad
☐ Sarcastic	☐ Sarcastic
☐ Mysterious	☐ Mysterious
☐ Scary	☐ Scary
☐ Other:	☐ Other:

Rewrite some of the lyrics, and spin the song with a new voice. The sentences do not have to rhyme, but be honest in how you feel about the topic, share what you really think, and use expressions to make a point. This is what writers do to develop a strong voice in their writing.

Strategy 11: Magnifying Glass

Student writers often have a difficult time sticking to the point. When given a prompt, they may write aimlessly without a clear idea of the information they want to communicate to their audience. The final product often contains too much nonessential material and not enough meaningful information. To help them establish focus in their writing, teach students to use Magnifying Glass.

1. Make copies of the magnifying glass (Figure 4.11.1) on cardstock paper.
2. Ask students to cut out the magnifying glass and the circle in the center.
3. Explain to students that they can bring the magnifying glass close to their eyes to reveal a wide image, or they can position the magnifying glass far from their eyes to focus on a much smaller area.
4. Have students practice manipulating the magnifying glass by first looking at a wide image (e.g., cars in the parking lot) and then focusing on a more detailed image (e.g., one particular car).
5. Point out that just as the magnifying glass helps them focus on different aspects of the world around them, it can also help them focus on their writing.
6. Assemble an exhibit, such as a box full of toys, an array of utensils, or a group of plants. Have students bring their magnifying glasses up to one of their eyes and describe what they see in the exhibit. They should provide a relatively wide perspective. Select one or two students' descriptions, and model how to write a descriptive paragraph. Then have students position their magnifying glasses away from their eyes and describe what they now see in the exhibit. They should provide more detailed descriptions. Model the writing again.
7. Use the T-chart (Figure 4.11.2) to discuss the differences between the two paragraphs.
8. Have students decide whether they want to bring the magnifying glass close to their eyes and write about the whole scene or move them away and write about a smaller—more isolated—image.

 Tip

Instead of exhibits, teachers can project photos or illustrations and allow students to use their magnifying glasses to view that format instead. In addition, teachers can take students outdoors and have them use their magnifying glasses to capture a broad image (e.g., a field of dandelions) or a more detailed image (e.g., a single dandelion).

Alternatives and Accommodations

- Allow students to draw the close-up image before writing about it. They can repeat with the broader image. Ask students to generate a list of adjectives that describe their drawings and then use those adjectives when they write.
- Prepare enough photographs to pass out so students can use them at their desks. This requires some preplanning, but using pictures that demonstrate a marked contrast in perspective will provide good examples for students.
- For students who are reluctant to write anything, this is a great assignment to separate into parts. Use the T-chart in a more structured way by numbering spaces in each column. Ask students to write just three ideas on each side of the chart. This will initiate the process and prompt them to think of words and simple ideas. Next, ask students to rewrite those ideas in complete sentences; encourage them to see that when they take small steps, they will start to see good results.

FIGURE 4.11.1 : Magnifying Glass

FIGURE 4.11.2 : T-Chart

T-Chart

Wide Image   Focused Image

Strategy 12: My Main Purpose

Student writers often have a hard time understanding that there can be several purposes for writing. In addition, they do not fully understand that they should focus their information according to their purpose. Consequently, they stick to a purpose they have used in the past and remember because it is familiar. With this strategy, you can expose students to five purposes for writing—to inform, explain, express, explore, and persuade—and help them refine their focus.

1. Using the My Main Purpose chart as a reference (Figure 4.12.1), review the various purposes for writing and examples of each. Elaborate with examples of your own, and explain that a piece of writing may contain more than one purpose.

2. Provide each student with a copy of the chart in Figure 4.12.2 and the prompt cards from Figure 4.12.3. Have students cut out the prompt cards.

3. Pick a prompt card, read it to the class, and explain why it should be pasted under the correct purpose column (i.e., To Inform, To Explain, etc.). If students read the prompts and don't understand the purpose, use Figure 4.12.1 to review.

4. Have students paste their copy of the card under the correct column.

5. Continue asking students to match a prompt card with the correct purpose until they are consistently correct.

6. Students should complete the chart independently.

7. If time remains, have students write their own examples for each purpose.

 ## Tip

Want to save paper? Project a blank chart on the board and add students' suggestions digitally. Students can also write their ideas themselves to complete the chart.

 ## Alternatives and Accommodations

- Let students work together with partners. One partner should state the purpose and the other should generate an example. The two students can alternate roles and help each other as needed.

- Use real-life writing examples that students would be likely to encounter. Cut out or print newspaper articles, research papers, "how-to" directions, or other examples of authentic writing. Have students match each to the appropriate purpose.

- Choose one purpose and provide several examples for just that one purpose. Then have students generate examples of their own that match that purpose. Proceed to the next purpose and repeat the process.

FIGURE 4.12.1 : My Main Purpose

To Inform	To Explain	To Express	To Explore	To Persuade
• to give knowledge of something • to give information (e.g., facts, news, data)	• to make something clear to someone • to make something understandable • to clear up meaning for someone	• to put one's thoughts or feelings into words • to reveal an emotion	• to search for something • to discover something • to examine a topic thoroughly	• to convince someone of something • to talk someone into something • to win someone over
"Let me give you a report with detailed information."	"Let me tell you how to _____ so you can understand clearly."	"Let me tell you about (or make up a story) about an experience."	"Let me write thoroughly about a topic I have researched or analyzed."	"Let me tell you my belief and talk you into agreeing with me."
Examples: • newspaper article • magazine article • business writing • informational brochure • lab report • summary	*Examples:* • "how-to" writing • step-by-step writing • lab experiment • procedure writing • explanatory writing • descriptive writing • clarification	*Examples:* • personal narrative • creative writing • feelings—emotions • thoughts—ideas • reaction to an experience	*Examples:* • research writing (paper) • "examining a topic" • analysis • open-ended response • evaluation report	*Examples:* • opinion paper • (one side; two sides; draw conclusion) • speech • movie review • book review • editorial • advertisement

FIGURE 4.12.2 : My Main Purpose Template

To Inform	To Explain	To Express	To Explore	To Persuade

FIGURE 4.12.3 : Prompt Cards

I have the best dog in the whole world.	Making a paper airplane is easy if you follow these steps.	Insulating a home is important for many reasons.	Animated movies are entertaining.	I started to cry when my bird died.
Let me tell you why my bike is a good buy.	On Saturday, my dad told me he was proud of me.	My experiment on sleep taught me a lot.	More and more children prefer chocolate milk.	My neighbor taught me how to make chocolate chip cookies.
Penguins are interesting.	Yesterday afternoon, I argued with my sister.	Taking care of plants requires a lot of work.	*High School Musical* is a great movie.	Breakfast is the most important meal of the day.
There are many benefits to wearing glasses.	I was terrified when I went to the doctor.	Everyone should read this book.	The Romans contributed so much to Western civilization.	Bees are fascinating insects.
Let me tell you about my trip to Washington, D.C.	Let me tell you about military working dogs.	Playing hopscotch can be fun if you remember these simple rules.	Here are some steps to follow when building a birdhouse.	

Strategy 13: Plan It Out

Teachers can never have too many tools for teaching writing. You might not need to use all of them all the time, but it is great to have several to choose from so you can meet individual students' needs and styles. The group of graphic organizers in this section, like others in this text, is intended to help students organize their thoughts and develop their ideas before they begin writing. Each graphic organizer is described below, along with directions for using it.

1. **Problem and Solution** (Figure 4.13.1): This organizer is intended for use when preparing to write about a problem and the associated solution(s). The first step is to ask students to identify the central problem. They can then add details about the problem, including the cause(s). To help with this, students should answer some basic questions (who, what, when, where, why, how). The next step is for students to propose a possible solution and supply details about it. Finally, at the bottom of the form, students can write their concluding thoughts. Make sure you teach and model how to use the form before expecting students to use it independently. For this writing, encourage students to propose solutions that are realistic and viable while still allowing for creative responses.

2. **Cause and Effect** (Figure 4.13.2): This form is simple to understand and simple to use. However, some students confuse causes and effects when they first start to write. Practice with some very concrete examples before students use the form as a prewriting tool. Students should first address the cause (or reason) for an event, action, or activity they are writing about. Next, students should brainstorm and write down ideas they have about possible effects. Students sometimes have difficulty with this step, so it might be helpful for them to work with a partner or small group as they think through possible effects and consequences. Finally, students should develop a concluding statement that summarizes their ideas about the cause-and-effect relationship and how it contributes to the topic as a whole.

3. **Climactic Order** (Figure 4.13.3): The type of composition for which this organizer is appropriate begins from the least important idea and builds toward the most important. For example, a student could write about a natural disaster by describing the tell-tale signs leading to the actual event. Have students write their ideas in the organizer, saving the "best for last," as it were.

4. **Reverse Climactic Order** (Figure 4.13.4): By contrast, this type of composition begins from the most important idea and descends to the least

important. For example, a student could write a mystery that begins with a tragic event and then describe the events that lead to it. Have students identify their ideas in the organizer, writing the most important at the top.

5. **Venn Diagram** (Figure 4.13.5): Venn diagrams are commonly used to compare and contrast a variety of ideas or subjects. Most students will already be familiar with Venn diagrams from other subject areas. To use a Venn diagram effectively, practice with students and be sure they understand how to move from a graphic that includes only the most salient similarities and differences to a more robust composition on the written page. Make sure students know whether they are focusing on similarities, differences, or both in their compositions.

Tip

The end goal of writing is not to complete graphic organizers; it's to write. When planning your lessons, make sure you allocate time so students spend more time writing than they do completing graphic organizers. The organizers are just tools and are not a substitute for practice.

Alternatives and Accommodations

- When helping young students understand and identify examples of cause and effect, try using a *"first . . . then"* approach. Ask, "What happened first? What happens next?" By getting the events in the correct sequence, students can more easily identify what is the cause and what is the effect.

- A key point to remember with graphic organizers is that they need to be simple. Even though your intention may be to help students use prewriting organizers as a way to get organized and stay focused, if the forms are too complicated, students will get bogged down and never complete the forms *or* the writing. Help students by asking them which forms they find most helpful and then sticking with what works. Sometimes, too many choices will just confuse them.

- As mentioned earlier, it may be helpful to use some of these forms in sections. For example, when using a Venn diagram, fold the paper in half lengthwise and complete one section at a time. Once the key facts or details for an object, person, or event have been described, turn the paper over and work on the other side. Finally, unfold the paper and add appropriate information to the overlapping central area, contrasting the two sides.

FIGURE 4.13.1 : Problem and Solution

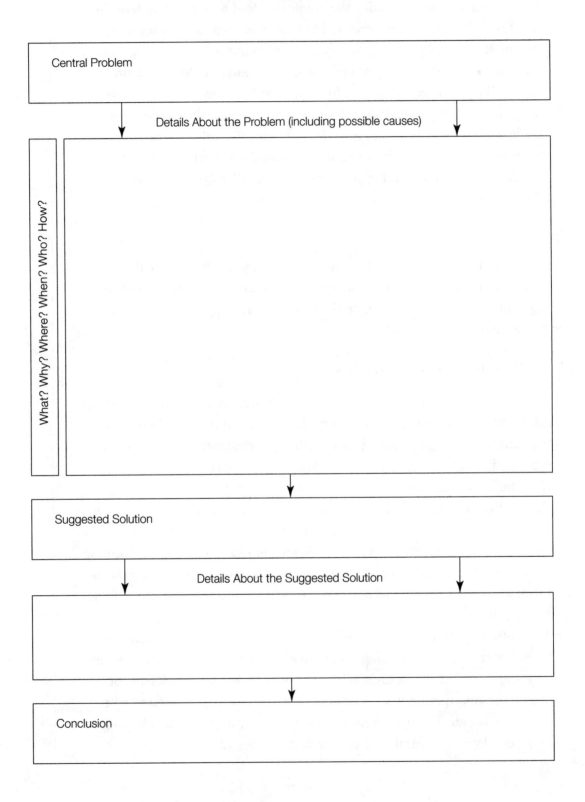

FIGURE 4.13.2 : **Cause and Effect**

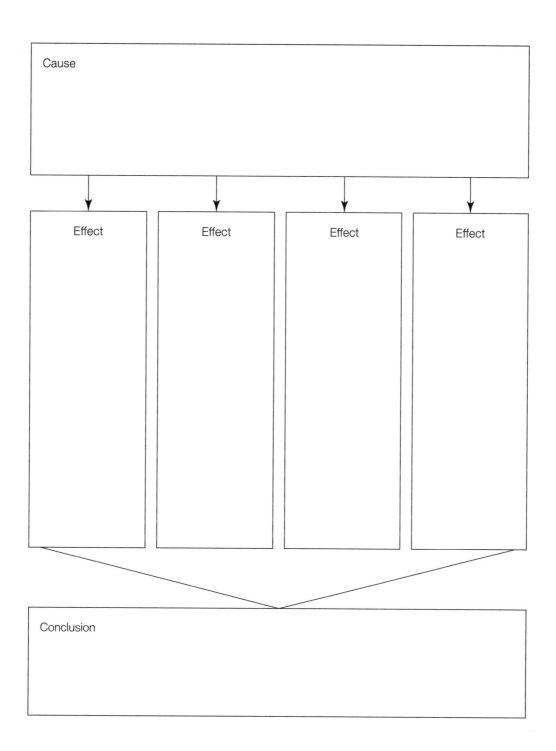

FIGURE 4.13.3 : Climactic Order

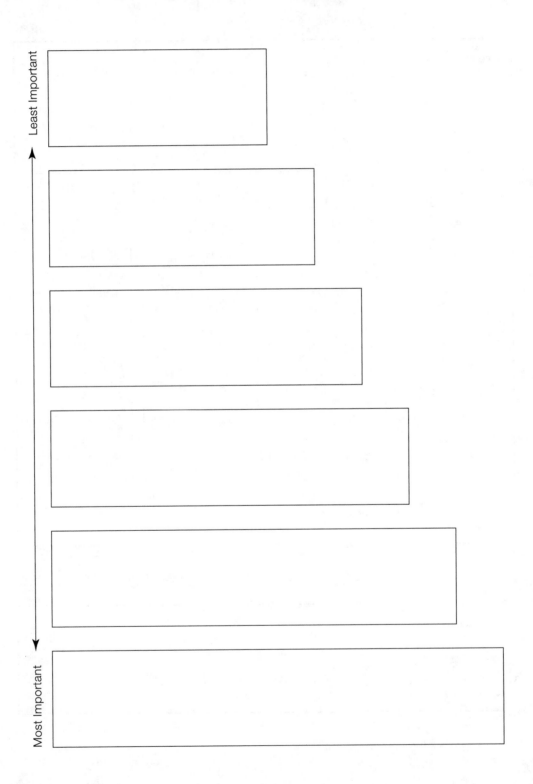

FIGURE 4.13.4 : Reverse Climactic Order

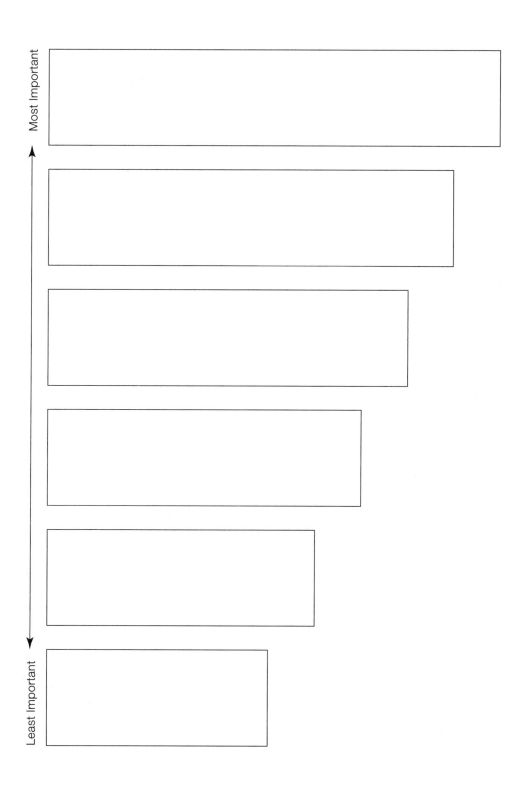

FIGURE 4.13.5 : Venn Diagram

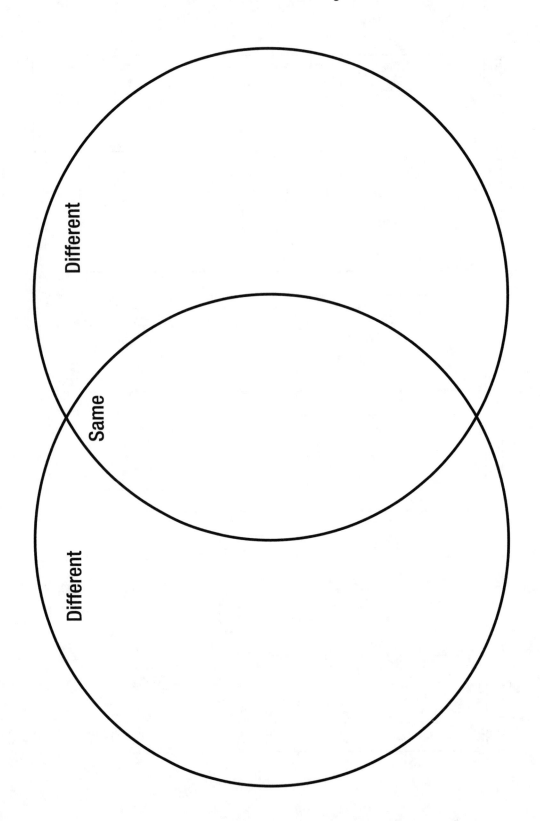

Strategy 14: Prewriting Pyramid

Struggling writers often omit three key steps during the writing process—the identification of prompt, purpose, and audience. When students are assigned a teacher-generated prompt or choose a prompt on their own, they frequently move directly to the brainstorming stage. This leap—from prompt to brainstorming—can result in a lack of focus and the use of irrelevant details in their writing. To help struggling writers clearly identify the important elements of prompt, purpose, and audience, students can use this strategy for any writing assignment.

1. Make a copy of the Prewriting Pyramid (Figure 4.14.1) for each student, and project a copy on the board for the whole class to see.

2. Copy the prewriting prompt cards (Figure 4.14.2), cut them apart, shuffle them, and place them in an envelope.

3. Have one student select a prompt card from the envelope. (Four of the prompt cards are intentionally left blank so you can write prompts that are individualized and relate to your students' ages, interests, and backgrounds.) He or she should read the prompt aloud, and then all students should paste it in the "Prompt" section of the pyramid.

4. Read aloud the associated question for this section on the pyramid: "What is it that I am being asked to do in my writing?"

5. Have students identify (by circling) key words and phrases in the prompt that answer this question.

6. Move to the "Purpose" section of the pyramid, and read aloud the associated question: "What is my reason for writing this piece?" Discuss the categories listed.

7. Ask students to identify the purpose that appropriately matches the writing prompt by checking its box.

8. Direct students' attention to the "Audience" section of the pyramid, and read aloud the associated question: "Who am I talking to with this writing?" Discuss the examples listed.

9. Have students brainstorm other possible audiences that might be appropriate for this writing task.

10. As a whole class, come to consensus on the most appropriate audience to whom this writing should be directed.

Tip

Color-code each section of the pyramid to mimic a traffic light. In other words, Prompt = red, Purpose = yellow, and Audience = green. This visual technique can help writers remember to "stop" and make sure they understand precisely what the prompt is asking them to do in their writing, "slow down" and identify the purpose that best fits the writing assignment, and "go" to the last stage of this prewriting process by identifying the appropriate audience.

Alternatives and Accommodations

- To support English language learners as they use this strategy, be sure to preteach the vocabulary that appears on the pyramid. Words such as *inform*, *persuade*, and *sibling* may not be familiar to some students. Explain the meanings of any unfamiliar words, provide examples, and then ask students to share their own examples so you can determine their level of understanding.

- To make sure that below-level readers can read and understand the prompts, select specific prompts that are simpler and at an appropriate reading level. You can also assign students to a small group in which all students write from the same prompt. Read the prompt aloud, and make sure students understand it before they begin to write.

- For students who find this activity challenging, first go through each of the prompt cards and focus on purpose. Once students can consistently identify the author's purpose, expand the lesson to include audience.

FIGURE 4.14.1 : **Prewriting Pyramid**

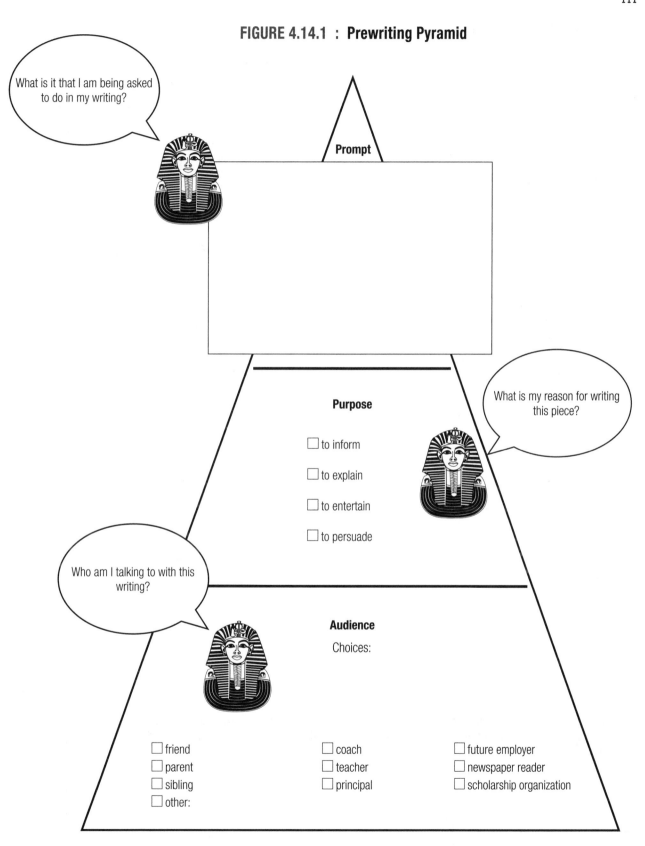

FIGURE 4.14.2 : Prewriting Prompt Cards

Attend a local high school football game, and interview the quarterback about what he does to stay in shape. Write a newspaper article for your school newspaper based on the interview.

Skim through a newspaper or magazine, and write a summary of one article you found interesting. Include the main idea and supporting details from the article.

Read a section of your science textbook that describes the life cycle of a particular type of animal, such as butterflies. Then write a one-page summary that includes specific details.

Conduct a science experiment on the effect of sunlight on a seedling's development. After you have completed the experiment and gathered information, write a one-page lab report that highlights your research results.

What is one possession you have that you cannot live without? Write a letter to your best friend and tell him or her why it is so important to you.

A television station is looking for ideas for a new music show for teenagers. Write a letter to the president of the station, and describe your idea for a new show.

Write a letter to your best friend in which you examine why you think honesty is an important quality for friends to have.

Write a letter to a pen pal in another country, and identify the characteristics of your hometown that make it a special place to live.

Think of the many experiences you have had and choose one experience that stands out as important. Write about this experience in a personal narrative.

Imagine that you are a new student in a new school. Write a letter to your best friend from your previous school, and tell him or her about your first day at the new school.

Write a journal entry about the most memorable moment of your life.

Think of a time you were in a major rainstorm that included thunder, lightning, and hurricane-like winds. Write a personal narrative for the weatherperson at your local TV station that recounts that experience.

Identify an American Indian group of your choice, and research information about them. Write an essay that describes important details about the group's lifestyle and beliefs.

Research ecofarming, and write a report that explains how and why the practice is important today.

Use the library, Internet, and other media to gather information on a famous American artist from the twentieth century. Write a report that you will present to a group of visiting artists from another country.

Research the details of the Lewis and Clark Expedition. Write a journal entry in which you document the events of a typical day for a member of the group.

(continued)

FIGURE 4.14.2 : **Prewriting Prompt Cards** (*continued*)

Write a speech to your classmates about the qualities you believe make a person honest.	Many teenagers think they are old enough to decide how late they can stay up at night. How do you feel about this issue? Write an editorial article for the local newspaper in which you try to influence readers to agree with you.
The local school board is trying to save money and has decided to increase class size. Write a letter to the school board defending your position (for or against) on this matter.	The city government is thinking about building a garbage landfill very close to your neighborhood. You do not believe this is a good idea. Write a formal letter to the city council in which you try to convince them to agree with you.

Source: Created by Susie Flatau. Adapted and reprinted with permission. The authors would like to thank Ms. Flatau for her contribution to this book.

Strategy 15: Questions to Clarify

Students' writing often lacks depth of thought, a sense of completeness, or fully developed ideas because they do not take the time to evaluate their writing critically. Teachers also have limited time to conference with individual students about their writing. This strategy, then, is ideal because students have to answer some tough questions about their writing and are accountable to their peers.

1. Break the class up into teams of four students each. Have students read one another's writing.

2. Assign each student (or let them choose) a number 1–4.

3. Provide each team with a spinner (with four sections) and a deck of Questions to Clarify cards (Figure 4.15.1). The questions on the cards will help students edit, revise, and improve their writing. One card is intentionally left blank so you can address specific issues that your students are having.

4. During each turn, one student draws a card, reads it out loud, and then spins the spinner. The number that the pointer lands on is the person to whom the question is directed. (The student should try again if the spinner stops on his or her number.) That student then responds to the question and then makes an appropriate edit, either orally or in writing. Finally, that student draws a new card, reads it out loud, and repeats the process.

5. Shuffle the cards so students can continue playing the game until everyone has answered at least four questions.

6. If a student cannot answer a question, encourage other group members to offer suggestions and support.

 ## Tip

Before breaking students into small groups, use the strategy for whole-group instruction. Project a writing sample for the class to see, have individual students choose a card, and then instruct them to make the appropriate edit.

 ## Alternatives and Accommodations

- If some English language learners are having difficulty understanding the clarifying questions or making changes to their writing, pair them with more proficient English-speaking students. As they work, partners can help each other by explaining the questions, peer editing, or both. Ask students to take turns answering the questions asked of their team.

- When students cannot read at the same level as their peers, they may be reluctant to participate in a group activity such as this one. They may have problems reading the questions or even reading their own writing. If this is the case, appoint one reader—a student who will read all of the questions—for each group. Students still spin to see who has to answer the question, but they don't have to read the question aloud.

- Some students get discouraged when work is challenging and they have to edit or correct mistakes. Because those two steps are part of this strategy, it is important to explain the process completely before starting. Make sure your students understand that others are not simply criticizing them; part of the writing process is to reflect, edit, and rewrite. Make sure you clarify rules and guidelines for how to ask clarifying questions respectfully.

FIGURE 4.15.1 : **Questions to Clarify Cards**

Clarify what you mean by _____ in the _____ paragraph.	Add a transition word to the _____ paragraph.
Provide an additional example in the _____ para-graph to support your main idea.	What evidence is there to support your conclusions?
Provide an additional detail in the _____ paragraph to support your main idea.	What leads you to believe the main point in the _____ paragraph?
Clarify your main point for the whole essay.	What leads you to believe the main point for the whole essay?
Clarify the main point in the _____ paragraph.	What are your reasons for saying _____ in the _____ paragraph?
Clarify the central theme about your topic.	What do you mean when you say _____ in the _____ paragraph?
Summarize the essay.	Why did you say _____ in the _____ paragraph?
How else might you say _____ in the _____ paragraph?	Give a deeper explanation for your point in the _____ paragraph.
Add a transition word to the _____ paragraph.	Use a more powerful verb in the _____ paragraph.
Use a word that paints a memorable picture in the _____ paragraph.	

Strategy 16: Revision Strips

Students can improve their writing through a variety of editing techniques, including adding, deleting, substituting, and rearranging words, sentences, and longer chunks of text. However, a difficulty student writers often encounter is that there are a seemingly infinite number of ways to use each technique. Revision Strips help students with the editing process because they encourage students to focus on a specific concept and edit their writing one concept at a time. For example, if students have been working on voice, then the editing process should focus on voice. Later, when students become more proficient writers, you can select an area to edit based on individual students' needs.

1. Make copies of the revision strips (Figure 4.16.1) for all students. Distribute one strip at a time.

2. Decide on a concept that you want to emphasize in writing. The concepts can range from using more descriptive words to expanding ideas with examples. At the top of the strip, have students write what they will focus on. Although you will usually want to assign the area of focus, you can let more experienced writers choose the topic themselves. Explain that they should look for ways to improve their compositions by adhering to a particular focus. An example is provided in Figure 4.16.2.

3. Direct students to read and reread their own papers, looking for specific ways to improve their writing. Explain to students that they can add, delete, substitute, or reorganize words, sentences, and paragraphs. After they have noted their proposed edits on the revision strips, consult with each student and check his or her ideas. If you approve, students can then make the appropriate corrections.

4. To improve their writing even more, students can solicit additional feedback from their peers. They should exchange papers in class and make suggestions in the respective boxes on the revision strips. If the writer agrees with the suggestions, he or she can then make those changes to the composition.

5. Give students another revision strip when it is time to focus their attention on another aspect of revision. Later, when students are comfortable with the strips, give several to each student so they are readily available during the writing, editing, and rewriting cycle.

Tip

Some students edit more effectively if they first highlight text. This strategy can be combined with highlighting by designating specific colors for specific types of revisions.

 Alternatives and Accommodations

- If students are struggling or unsuccessful with self-editing, provide multiple opportunities to edit the same passage. Explain to students that professional writing often gets edited numerous times, not just once. The quality of the writing often improves with each pass an editor makes!

- It is always a good idea to model and provide guided practice with a new technique before expecting students to use it independently. When teaching students to use the revision strips, distribute the same composition to the entire class and model the editing process for everyone. Then assign students a specific aspect to edit and, again, let all students edit the same piece of writing. Students can compare their edits and support their decisions. This type of discussion will help less-confident writers hear and better understand the "why" and "how" steps of the process.

- Students who are having difficulty with writing may not recognize when they need to change something in their writing, even if you make specific suggestions. For these students, use the revision strips as a conferencing tool. Explain what you are going to look for in their writing, and then use a think-aloud process while you edit. Talk to students as you read and edit, explaining why you are suggesting (or making) specific changes.

FIGURE 4.16.1 : Revision Strips

Focus on: _____

1) Read and reread

	Add	
◯		
◯	Delete	
◯	Substitute	
◯	Reorganize	

2) Ask for feedback

	Add	
◯		
◯	Delete	
◯	Substitute	
◯	Reorganize	

Focus on: _____

1) Read and reread

	Add	
◯		
◯	Delete	
◯	Substitute	
◯	Reorganize	

2) Ask for feedback

	Add	
◯		
◯	Delete	
◯	Substitute	
◯	Reorganize	

FIGURE 4.16.2 : Revision Strips Example

Focus on: _Organization_

1) Read and reread 2nd paragraph

○	Add	
✓	Delete	the last sentence
○	Substitute	
✓	Reorganize	move the first sentence to the end

2) Ask for feedback from Joe

✓	Add	more details about the dog
○	Delete	
○	Substitute	
○	Reorganize	

Focus on: _Voice_

1) Read and reread 3rd & 4th paragraphs

✓	Add	figurative language about about the character
○	Delete	
○	Substitute	
○	Reorganize	

2) Ask for feedback from Sophie

○	Add	
○	Delete	
✓	Substitute	use an idiom instead of a simile
○	Reorganize	

Strategy 17: Rich Language Generator

Students' writing can sometimes get boring and dull because they have a difficult time mastering the use of descriptive language. This strategy is a great way to enhance students' use of original expressions.

1. Find an appropriate picture to serve as a writing prompt, and project it during instruction.
2. Provide students with a copy of the Rich Language Generator form (Figure 4.17.1).
3. Explain the importance of using rich words and phrases to create meaning and engage readers.
4. Ask students to explain what they see in the picture. You can focus on the background, foreground, small features, large features, or any object or element. For instance, you can say, "I want you to focus your attention on the background. Describe what you see." Or, "Now, let's look at the house. What do you see?"
5. Have students use the form to write exactly what they see. (Distribute Figure 4.17.2 if students need to see some examples.)
   - In the first column, students should name the object they are focusing on.
   - In the second column, ask students to list features of the object.
   - In the third column, students should write what the object resembles. This is also a good place to review similes and metaphors.
   - In the final column, have students brainstorm ideas about how the object might seem if it were human.
   - Finally, have students combine their ideas and images into a descriptive sentence that describes the object.
6. Repeat the process as many times as you feel is appropriate.
7. Have students share their sentences and display them on the whiteboard so the whole class sees many different examples. Students can even vote for their favorites.

 Tip

The Rich Language Generator form can be used in different ways. You may want to have students write sentences on entirely different topics just to practice their figurative language. Alternatively, their sentences can all relate to one topic and be used in one paragraph. (Of course, this paragraph will need other types of sentences to be complete.)

Alternatives and Accommodations

- Keep in mind that students from diverse cultures may respond differently or not relate at all to some photos, especially when the photos are of unfamiliar objects, places, or people. As you select photographs to share as prompts for this activity, make sure you introduce them to your students and allow students to ask questions they might have about them. If you find that some students are so puzzled by a photograph that using it as a writing prompt would be counterproductive, then select an alternative photo for students to describe.

- Writing sentences and compositions that contain imagery may seem very stilted or artificial at first. To help students get more comfortable with using imagery in their writing, consider sharing high-quality examples of students' writing without revealing the author. Read the writing samples aloud, pointing out the positive uses of imagery.

- Some aspects of this activity might be more difficult than others. For example, the third column, which requires students to identify other things that the object resembles, might be challenging for students who are more concrete thinkers. For these students, provide support by using sentence frames such as "The _____ looks like a _____" or "The _____ is as big as a _____." If you prepare these cues ahead of time, it will be easier to help students when they become stumped and can't think of what to write.

FIGURE 4.17.1 : Rich Language Generator

The object	Features of the object	The object resembles . . .	If the object were human, it would seem . . .

String the images together into a complete descriptive sentence:

The object	Features of the object	The object resembles . . .	If the object were human, it would seem . . .

String the images together into a complete descriptive sentence:

The object	Features of the object	The object resembles . . .	If the object were human, it would seem . . .

String the images together into a complete descriptive sentence:

FIGURE 4.17.2 : Rich Language Generator Examples

The object	Features of the object	The object resembles . . .	If the object were human, it would seem . . .
hay fields	• in rows • waist-high • yellow • The wind is blowing through it.	• gold • a lion's mane • spaghetti • gold chains	• free spirited • relaxed • well rested • caressed by the wind

String the images together into a complete descriptive sentence:

The gold hay fields that are caressed by the wind look free spirited and relaxed.

The object	Features of the object	The object resembles . . .	If the object were human, it would seem . . .
the sky	• strikingly blue • cloud free • Black birds are flying in it.	• the sea	• happy • blissful • peppy

String the images together into a complete descriptive sentence:

The strikingly blue sky enjoyed the company of flying crows.

The object	Features of the object	The object resembles . . .	If the object were human, it would seem . . .
a cart	• brown and gray • red wheels • wooden • long • old	• junk • firewood thrown together • a neglected, worn-out tool	• sad • depressed • somber • to be wanting someone's attention

String the images together into a complete descriptive sentence:

The brown and gray wooden cart was neglected and yearned for attention.

Strategy 18: Sentence Search

Student writers can improve the quality of their writing when they use the four different kinds of sentences—declarative, imperative, exclamatory, and interrogative—throughout their writing. This strategy is a useful tool to help students recognize the types of sentences they are using, and it prompts them to adjust sentence types to improve variety and the complexity of their writing. Before beginning the activity, make sure all of your students understand and can identify each kind of sentence.

1. Have students work in pairs for this activity. If you have a diverse class, this is a good opportunity to assign partners based on mixed abilities, varied learning styles, or other relevant factors. Assign each partner a number: either 1 or 2.

2. Make a copy of the Sentence Search cards (Figure 4.18.1) for each pair of students.

3. Instruct students to cut out the cards, shuffle them, and organize them face down into two separate piles—one with the words in all lowercase letters and one with the words in all capital letters. You can also color-code the cards by copying them onto colored paper and organizing them in stacks by color.

4. Provide students with an appropriate, on-level selection from a short story, novel, newspaper or magazine article, or content-area textbook. Have students skim through the passage so they are familiar with it. (When selecting a passage for this activity, short stories and novels will probably be best because they usually have the widest variety of sentence types. Try to plan ahead and find a passage with several different types of sentences.)

5. After students have had an opportunity to skim and familiarize themselves with the reading passage, they can begin to use the Sentence Search cards. Each Student 1 should pick a card from one stack and locate a sentence in the passage that matches that type. He or she should then pick a card from the other stack and attempt to change the sentence so that it represents that new sentence type.

   For example, if Karina chooses a "declarative" card, she looks for and finds one that reads, "The whole village went down to the sea when the fishermen came back in their boats." Encourage students to read their sentences aloud. Next, Karina picks a card from the other stack. She chooses "INTERROGATIVE." Therefore, she needs to change the sentence into a question, such as "What did the villagers do when the fishermen came back in their boats?"

6. Finally, both cards are placed into "discard" piles, and Student 2 repeats the process. If there is no sentence in the passage that matches the type indicated on a card (or if a student chooses two cards that indicate the same sentence type), then the student simply draws a new card. Students should continue to shuffle the "discard" pile cards back into the main piles to ensure variety in the activity.

7. After students have played this game with an assigned reading selection that someone else has written, they should then use their own compositions for the game. After drawing a card, students must find a sentence of the type indicated on the card or make up a new sentence they can include in their writing to make it more meaningful. Partners should be encouraged to offer each other constructive feedback in the process.

 Tip

Not all sentences can be easily transformed from one type (e.g., declarative) to another (e.g., imperative). Therefore, consider making a "joker card" that allows students to skip sentences that are difficult to change.

 Alternatives and Accommodations

- Remember to provide visual cues for students who need them. By adding the appropriate end punctuation marks onto the cards, you can help students remember what long words such as *interrogative* mean. (Of course, you'll also need to explain that a period could indicate either a declarative or an imperative sentence). This way, students won't get stuck on the meanings and can instead focus on finding and creating sentences.

- Consider providing individual sentences instead of a long passage. Students can still change sentences from one type to another, but they will be less likely to get bogged down in the reading.

- This activity could also be completed orally. Instead of finding a sentence in the passage, allow students to generate a sentence and say it out loud.

FIGURE 4.18.1 : Sentence Search Cards

declarative	declarative	DECLARATIVE	DECLARATIVE
imperative	imperative	IMPERATIVE	IMPERATIVE
exclamatory	exclamatory	EXCLAMATORY	EXCLAMATORY
interrogative	interrogative	INTERROGATIVE	INTERROGATIVE

Strategy 19: Sequence Cards

Some student writers struggle with how to connect ideas from paragraph to paragraph. Consequently, their writing suffers because their ideas shift throughout their compositions. This constant shifting of ideas makes it difficult for readers to understand the relationship of one idea to another. Other times, students do not sequence events in a logical order. This lack of a coherent sequence makes it difficult for readers to follow and understand what the writer is trying to say because it doesn't make sense. To help students improve the trait of coherence, consider using sequence cards. These cards allow for manipulation so students can focus their attention on what they want to say and when they should say it.

1. Make and distribute a copy of the sequence cards (Form 4.19.1) to each student. Explain that they will have one "opener" card and several "paragraph" cards.

2. On the opener card, have students identify the overall topic of their essay and the major supporting details that will serve as the framework for their writing.

3. On each paragraph card, students should write the main idea of the paragraph, along with supporting details they will develop into related sentences. It will help most students if you model this step with an example of your own writing or a familiar piece of text.

4. Students can then cut out the cards and arrange them in whatever sequence they believe makes for a strong piece of writing.

5. Have students work together to discuss why they arranged their paragraphs accordingly, and then solicit their feedback.

6. Once they have finalized the order, have them number the paragraphs and then begin writing.

 ## Tip

Ask students to create a simple timeline of events before they begin writing. A simple, straight line that is labeled with a beginning, an end, and keywords such as *first*, *second*, and *finally*, can help students get organized.

Alternatives and Accommodations

- If using the cards is too abstract for some students, begin with an outline. The outline can consist of individual words or short phrases that help students keep their ideas in order.

- Some students may need to use a visual such as a web to organize their ideas before using the sequence cards. Help them focus each paragraph on a specific subtopic that is related to the overall topic and main idea.

- For students who have difficulty writing anything longer than a few sentences, begin this activity with just the opener paragraph. Slowly add paragraphs as students become familiar with the process. To help students write multiparagraph compositions, suggest topics that are very familiar and lend themselves to a concrete method of organization. Keep in mind that even though some topics are appropriate for many students, the key to differentiation is to take a step-by-step approach. For example, students could write:

  - An essay that explains an activity or event in a timeline or sequence, such as an autobiography, a chronology of events that happen during the school year, or a descriptive essay that explains how the landscape changes with the seasons.

  - A story that provides a basic description of the characters and setting, beginning events, a rising action, a climax, and a conclusion or lesson learned. One way to do this would be to take a classic story and "modernize" it.

  - A composition that describes several characteristics or features of a person, place, or thing. Students could write a descriptive essay about members of their family, places in their neighborhood, their friends, or their favorite hobbies.

  - An essay that addresses several different arguments and persuasions. For example, students could argue for or against the benefits of specific electronic devices.

FIGURE 4.19.1 : **Sequence Cards**

Essay Topic: The supporting details are: 1. 2. 3.	Introductory Paragraph Card
The main idea of this paragraph is: _____ _____ The supporting details are: 1. 2. 3.	Paragraph Card
The main idea of this paragraph is: _____ _____ The supporting details are: 1. 2. 3.	Paragraph Card
The main idea of this paragraph is: _____ _____ The supporting details are: 1. 2. 3.	Paragraph Card

Strategy 20: Soccer, Anyone?

Student compositions often cause readers to lose interest because there is no clear focus. Instead, ideas are jumbled together with no real direction or clarity. To help students establish a clear central theme about the topic, consider using a soccer ball as a prewriting activity.

1. Make a copy of Figure 4.20.1 for each student.
2. Tell students that this activity is intended to help them identify a topic or theme and stick to it when they write. Ask each student to identify his or her topic or theme and write it at the goal post at the top of the page.
3. Students can brainstorm ideas related to the topic and write them in the hexagons on the soccer ball, one idea per space. Encourage students to fill as many hexagons as possible.
4. When they are finished recording their ideas, tell them to reread what they have written in the hexagons and ask themselves, "Is this related to my topic?" If the sentence is related to the topic, ask them to leave it on the soccer ball. If it is not, they should cross it out.
5. Ask students to write a sentence that describes the main idea (i.e., the central idea that captures what is written in the ball) in the "goal post" at the bottom of the page.
6. Later, as students begin writing, remind them that their ideas support the goal, which is the central theme of the paper (or paragraph).

Tip

One fun way to "hook" your students with this strategy is to adapt it into a whole-class activity. Give students a topic and ask them to generate and write ideas on separate sticky notes. Pass a real soccer ball around and as each student gets the ball, he or she can attach an idea to it. (Alternatively, students could write their ideas on the ball with dry-erase markers.) After students cover the ball with ideas, read the ideas aloud, decide if they address the main idea, and model how to write the paragraph.

Alternatives and Accommodations

- After identifying a topic with students, fill in a soccer ball with some ideas that relate to the topic and some ideas that do not. Ask students to cut the hexagons apart and sort them into two piles: ideas that relate to the topic and ideas that do not.

- You can supply three or four details in the hexagons, ask your students to suggest a main idea sentence, and then have them complete the rest of the hexagons.
- Some students will get overwhelmed when they see all of the blank hexagons. For those students, highlight some of the shapes and have students begin by writing ideas in those sections only. This will help them get started. You can add additional sections after they complete the first group.

FIGURE 4.20.1 : Soccer Ball Pattern

"My topic is _____ "

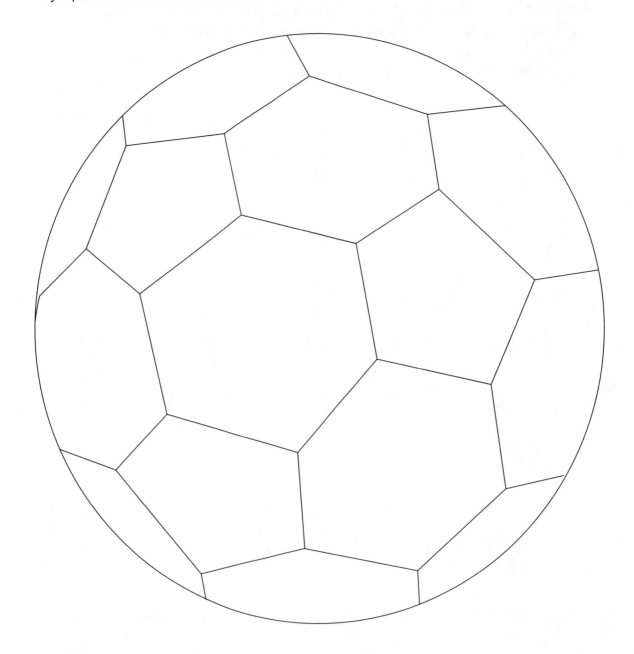

"My topic sentence is _____ "

Strategy 21: Speech Bubbles

Good writers have a way of eliciting a strong response from their readers. Their voice is often unique and personal, and their convictions are evident through their choice of words. One way to get students to think about the power of voice is to read a passage with simple and uninteresting language and then reread the same passage after it has been enriched with active words, original phrases, and language that expands ideas. In this strategy, students use speech bubbles to liven up passages that might be dull and boring.

1. Find about a dozen post cards, magazine photos, political cartoons, and comic strips to show students. Remove or cover up any writing that might appear. Project the remaining image on the board.

2. Copy and cut out different speech bubbles (Figure 4.21.1).

3. Explain to students that a writer's voice has to engage the reader's interest and that this can be done with words that figuratively "paint" memorable pictures.

4. Model language in the speech bubbles that does not engage the reader. For instance, in a cartoon that depicts children watching TV, talking on their cell phones, or using the Internet, use simple language, such as "I like to watch TV," "Talking to my friends is fun," or "I love my Facebook account." Then substitute the speech bubbles with others that have more engaging language: "The actors in my favorite show won awards for their performance," "My friends and I are like peas in a pod," "It's comforting to know that my social network is expanding." Explain that in the new speech bubbles, the reader is more engaged and wants to know more. They might be asking themselves, "What actors? What show?" "Why is her social network expanding?" and "Why are they so close?"

5. Hand out copies of the speech bubbles to each student. Organize students into pairs and give each an appropriate image (e.g., photo, cartoon, or comic strip). Then challenge students to create speech bubbles that are filled with rich and precise language that is strong, striking, energetic, and active.

6. Have the whole class share their images and associated speech bubbles.

 ## Tip

Students can do before-and-after speech bubbles that show the difference between dull and engaging. Award a prize to the most creative speech bubbles.

Alternatives and Accommodations

- Vocabulary knowledge is a major part of this strategy. For English language learners, it might be necessary to use flash cards to help them learn and remember synonyms or substitute phrases. For example, if students are trying to think of words or phrases that convey a specific meaning, brainstorm synonyms as a group, write each one on a card, and then arrange the cards by intensity or shades of meaning. Allow students to refer to these cards during the activity.

- For this and similar activities, students may benefit from access to a word bank or picture dictionary. They can create these themselves, with teacher support, or you can make suitable versions available in print or electronic format. The first few times you use this strategy, allow students to use their word banks and dictionaries, but gradually try to reduce their dependence on these resources so they gain confidence and can complete the activity on their own.

- Sometimes, students can get stuck and use the same words over and over. To help students branch out and find their own voice when they write, consider using cloze (fill-in-the-blank) sentences. Remove words from various sentences and ask students to suggest a word or phrase they have not used before to fill in the blank.

FIGURE 4.21.1 : Speech Bubbles

Strategy 22: Spin Your Point of View

Many times, students write with a point of view that is familiar to them: their own. To help them reduce this tendency and develop the skill of writing from a different point of view, they'll obviously need to practice *using* other points of view. To help students write from another's point of view, they may need to pretend to be someone else—a different character in a story, someone who participates in an event, and so forth.

1. Project the game board (Figure 4.22.1) so all students can see it.
2. Cut out the spinner (Figure 4.22.2) and attach a spinner arrow. (You can purchase one or make your own with a paper clip.)
3. At the top of the board, write the topic or prompt that you want students to write about. Choose a topic you know will generate differing opinions and points of view among your students. For instance, you could write:
   • Should we have shorter school weeks with more hours in each day?
   • Should we stop offering fattening foods in the cafeteria?
   • Is the character of Cinderella a heroine or a victim?
   • Is it good for students to work together in school, or should students do all of their work alone?
   • Should our country stop using fossil fuels such as oil for energy and instead use renewable resources such as wind and solar energy?
4. In the first row (with the numbered write-on lines), write the different points of view that you want students to consider. For instance, if the topic is about a shorter school week, you could write "students," "teachers," "parents," and "community members" in those spaces. If cafeteria food is the topic, then you might write "cafeteria manager," "students," "principals," and "doctors" in those spaces.
5. Call on a student to spin the spinner. Whatever number the spinner lands on is the point of view that student has to express. Have that student contribute a sentence to the topic from the appropriate point of view. Suggest to students that they contribute a main idea statement about the position they are taking. You can follow up with questions that elicit supporting details or reasons why the student holds the opinion he or she does. If necessary, lead students with a question such as the following:
   • "What would _____ say about _____?"
   • "How do you suppose _____ feels about _____?"
   • "How does _____ benefit from _____?"

6. Continue calling on students and spinning the spinner until the entire game board is filled in. For more than four points of view, use an additional game board and call on students randomly. (However, we do not recommend more than four as it might confuse students). Follow up by explaining that in order to keep a consistent point of view in their writing, students should stick to ideas that are related to the same person (i.e., the same point of view). They can even cut out or highlight one column and only look at that one when they write.

7. Have students choose a column and begin writing a draft of their papers. Alternatively, you can choose to provide more practice by playing another game with a different topic.

 ## Tip

When suggesting topics, questions, or scenarios, first use those that will elicit strong and clearly different points of view (e.g., dress codes in schools) and work toward more subtle variations of opinion (e.g., good manners when texting). However, remind students to be respectful and refrain from insulting or prejudicial comments.

 ## Alternatives and Accommodations

- You might need to help some students understand point of view by using some specific phrases as cues or prompts. For example, if students are having problems with this activity, ask them to begin each sentence with the phrase "If I were _____, I would think _____ and say _____." Use this prompt when the student shifts to a different point of view or each time the student is ready to write another sentence or paragraph.

- For students who have problems shifting from one point of view to another, mount appropriate pictures, faces, or name cards on craft sticks. When a student needs to contribute from a specific point of view, he or she selects that name card or picture, holds it up, and then answers. This visual cue might help students remember whose point of view they are supposed to be representing.

- Rather than ask all students to play the game and contribute sentences that reflect various points of view, some students can instead focus on just one point of view. When it is their turn to participate, they can (instead of spinning) offer ideas that relate just to one person and his or her point of view.

FIGURE 4.22.1 : Spin Your Point of View Game Board

Topic:			
1_____	2_____	3_____	4_____

FIGURE 4.22.2 : Spin Your Point of View Spinner

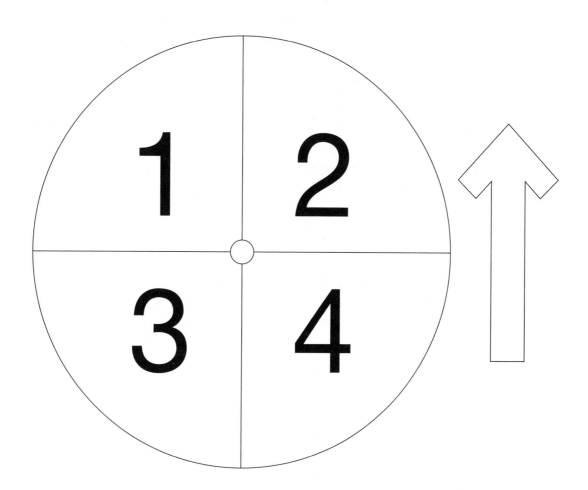

Strategy 23: Split Voice

The voice a writer uses conveys meaning through a variety of language conventions, figurative details, and specific techniques such as dialogue and pacing. With instruction, guidance, and practice, students can improve their writer's voice and make their compositions stand out.

When you teach students and then allow opportunities for peer feedback, students can develop their own sense of voice. They can learn to write in their own style while using meaningful and expressive language. Split Voice is a writing strategy that can be used during a think-pair-share activity to help students develop a strong voice that is appropriate to their topic, audience, and purpose. In this activity, students have an opportunity to examine a single topic presented in different ways.

1. Distribute the Split Voice form (Figure 4.23.1) to pairs of students.
2. Have students write the topic of their writing in the center block. (Each student should be writing about the same topic.)
3. Have one partner identify an audience and a purpose for writing, along with the voice they plan to use (e.g., humorous, disappointed, etc.), and then write those at the top of the left-hand column. If students have difficulty identifying a voice, review options with them. Some examples are provided in Figure 4.10.2 (pages 91–92).
4. Have the other partner do the same but with a different audience, purpose for writing, and voice. He or she should write those at the top of the right-hand column. Make sure your students understand that even though they will both write on the same topic, each should approach that topic from a different angle. As students work together, instruct them to discuss with their partner what audience, purpose, and voice they intend to use before they begin to write. Otherwise, they both may take the same approach.
5. Students can then write sentences from the different perspectives they each identified. They can cut the paper in half if it makes the activity easier for them to complete.
6. After some guided practice, have students exchange their papers and comment how additional expressions could arouse similar feelings in the reader. If students need some guidelines for reviewing and commenting on each other's work appropriately, you could easily provide some key components to look for in each other's writing. Students should identify specific words, phrases, and language usage that express a specific voice.
7. Give students a set amount of time to write and edit their drafts.

Tip

Provide students with a list of topics that can be written about from different perspectives. For example, students could write about the following prompts:

- How kids should respond to teasing.
- How it feels when your favorite team loses a game.
- What it's like to meet a new person.
- What it might be like to travel to an exotic location.

 Alternatives and Accommodations

- Topics that are familiar, are age appropriate, and lend themselves to different perspectives should work best with English language learners. Consider relevant topics such as "adapting to life in a new country."
- Some students will need concrete examples of words and phrases that change the voice of a composition. To share these, present a sentence in one voice and then another. Point out the differences and highlight the language used to change the voice. Next, show students some sentences and, as a whole group, ask them to suggest changes that will impact the voice of the composition. After students have had practice in the group, they may do better on their own.
- To help students complete the activity, consider allowing them to take a step-by-step approach. For example, Student A writes one sentence, and Student B then writes it in a different voice. Then have them switch: Student B should write a sentence, and Student A rewrites it. This may be more effective than expecting partners to complete the entire assignment independent of each other.

FIGURE 4.23.1 : Split Voice

Topic: _____

Audience: _____

Purpose: _____

Voice: _____

◆ Be Honest   ◆ Use Expression   ◆ Share What You Think

Audience: _____

Purpose: _____

Voice: _____

◆ Be Honest   ◆ Use Expression   ◆ Share What You Think

Strategy 24: Stick to the Point

Good writers achieve clear focus when they know what they want to write about. Their essays and stories have a central idea or controlling theme, and their supporting points are clear to the reader. In this strategy, students narrow down what they want to write about and how they want to write about it. In the process, they get some guidance from their peers and teacher.

1. Give each student a copy of the Stick to the Point form (Figure 4.24.1).
2. Have students indicate what they want to write about on top of the form. They can then indicate their purpose for writing and the central theme of their story or essay.
3. Provide time to reflect on the supporting sentences that contribute to the central theme. Students can then write the supporting sentences on the left side of the T-chart.
4. Break the class into small groups, and ask each student to offer at least one supporting sentence central to his or her peer's theme. Peers' sentences should be written on the right side of the T-chart.
5. Offer your own recommendations on the bottom of the form.
6. When the form is complete, students are ready to begin a first draft.

 ## Tip

This form can be used for a single paragraph or to help organize a complete essay. If used for an entire essay, make sure students organize their sentences into paragraphs before beginning to write.

 ## Alternatives and Accommodations

- If students are stuck and cannot think of a topic, provide some prompts. Try using visuals and real objects as prompts. Photographs, drawings, and tangible objects may help English language learners avoid the limitations that written prompts bring to those who are unfamiliar with the language.
- When assigning students to small groups, you may want to group together three to five students with similar reading levels. We often suggest more heterogeneous grouping strategies, but in this activity, it may help students if they can discuss and work on one another's ideas at the same level. Students can also work together to write one passage instead of individual passages. They can each contribute a few sentences and when they are finished, they will have a solid paragraph or theme.

- Monitor struggling students closely as they write their sentences. Remind students to ask themselves if each sentence they write is related to the central theme of their writing. If it is not, ask them to try again.

FIGURE 4.24.1 : **Stick to the Point**

Here is what I want to write about:

_____

My purpose is to:

_____

My central theme is:

_____

Here are my supporting sentences that contribute to my central theme:	Here are my peers' supporting sentences that contribute to my central theme:

Here are my teacher's recommendations:

_____

_____

Strategy 25: Three Tab POV

Some students fail to keep a consistent point of view in their writing. They may alternate between the first and third person or shift perspectives repeatedly throughout a composition. These shifts can be distracting to readers. Therefore, students need to learn to maintain a consistent point of view throughout their sentences, paragraphs, and compositions.

To promote consistency, consider using this strategy, which helps keep students on track and allows them to compare and contrast how different points of view can be used in their writing. Before beginning the activity, make sure your students know which pronouns and nouns are used with each point of view. Review the Pronoun Consistency list with students (Figure 4.25.1), and suggest that they refer to them as needed while writing.

1. In this strategy, students will create a three-tab foldable using Figure 4.25.2.
2. Copy the Three Tab POV form for each student. Have students fold the form in half horizontally and cut along the dotted lines. This should make a three-tab foldable. Students should be able to lift the tabs labeled "1st Person," "2nd Person," and "3rd Person."
3. Discuss first-person point of view and the pronouns associated with it.
4. Ask each student to generate sentences using first-person point of view. Students should write these sentences under the "1st Person" tab. Have them repeat this step for second-person and third-person points of view.
5. After students have had some time to practice writing in one specific point of view, make sure they can use the same point of view consistently when writing an entire paragraph. To do this, ask students to select a topic, choose a point of view, and write a five-sentence paragraph that uses that point of view consistently. They can create a second POV foldable to help them with this paragraph.

Tip

Explain to students that second-person point of view is not commonly used. This point of view may weaken writing because it sounds as if the writer is constantly offering advice or telling the reader what to do.

Alternatives and Accommodations

- Partner English language learners with students whose English language skills are stronger. Because original writing requires a high level of language competency, pairing English language learners with native English speakers can help support the former with grammar, spelling, mechanics, and other basics.
- For students who find the foldable confusing, allow them to write their sentences on sentence strips labeled with a 1, 2, or 3 (to indicate point of view). When they are finished writing their sentences, they can ask a peer to check their work.
- Provide students with completed sentences, and have them paste those sentences under the correct tab.

FIGURE 4.25.1 : Pronoun Consistency

Voice	First Person	Second Person	Third Person
Who?	The speaker The writer	The listener The reader	Everyone else
Pronouns	• *I, me, my, mine, myself* • *we, us, our, ours, ourselves*	• *you, your, yours, yourself*	• *he, him, his, himself* • *she, her, hers, herself* • *it, its, itself* • *they, them, their, theirs, themselves* • *the dog, Dr. Smith, etc.*
Examples	• I love my cat Ralph. • I find Anthony Hopkins to be a charismatic speaker. • We were exhausted from the long hike.	• You get the juice from the refrigerator. • (You) Write this down. • You find the strange smell disturbing.	• My cat Ralph is adorable. • Anthony Hopkins is a charismatic speaker. • The long hike was tiring.

FIGURE 4.25.2 : Three Tab POV

POINT OF VIEW	POINT OF VIEW	POINT OF VIEW
1st Person	2nd Person	3rd Person
the speaker, the writer	the listener, the reader	Everyone except the speaker/writer and listener/reader
• *I, me, my, mine, myself* • *we, us, our, ours, ourselves*	*you, your, yours, yourself*	• *he, him, his, himself* • *she, her, hers, herself* • *it, its, itself* • *they, them, their, theirs, themselves* • *the dog, Dr. Smith, etc.*

Strategy 26: Topic Sentence Development

Students often have a difficult time developing topic sentences because they are overwhelmed with what they want to say, and they don't understand that one lead sentence (i.e., the topic sentence) unifies all of the others that follow. A graphic organizer can help them visually discern how a topic sentence sets the scope of an entire paragraph (or essay) and how the other sentences should relate to it.

Before implementing this strategy, make sure you have done a thorough and effective job of teaching students how to write a topic sentence. Depending on your students' ages and writing skills, some may need a quick review, whereas others may have to be taught more thoroughly. If you find that your students do not know how to write good topic sentences, consider using some or all of these steps: (a) explain the characteristics of a good topic sentence; (b) model or demonstrate how to write good topic sentences from ideas, details, or supporting sentences; (c) give your students guided practice; (d) provide feedback through editing (teacher and peer), conferencing, and self-reflection; and (e) provide opportunities for independent practice and additional feedback. Throughout the process, continually check for understanding and demonstration of mastery.

1. Give each student a copy of Figure 4.26.1.
2. Read the three statements about topic sentences aloud.
3. After students have selected a topic and brainstormed ideas, ask them to write their own topic sentence in the first box.
4. Explain that subsequent sentences should be details about the topic sentence and should all relate to the topic sentence.
5. Instruct students to write their supporting sentences.

 Tip

After students have written their topic sentences, provide them with the questions at the bottom of Figure 4.1.1 (page 38). If they can answer "yes" to all of these questions, then they have probably written a strong, coherent topic sentence. If they have answered "no" to any of the questions, then they need to revise.

 Alternatives and Accommodations

- While it may seem obvious what the topic of a paragraph is when reading, it can be a real challenge for students to generate and write a topic sentence on their own. For English language learners, it is important to discuss the topic before they start writing. If they can't tell you what their main idea is, then they will not be able to write about the idea. Therefore, focus on brainstorming first and, if possible, conduct a one-on-one discussion so they are perfectly clear about their main idea.

- Guide below-grade-level readers to write what they know. Help them pick a topic that they know something about, feel comfortable with, and can discuss easily. When students try to write about something unfamiliar, the process usually does not go well. Work with students to think of topics related to activities they enjoy, places they have been, people they know, and situations they find interesting. Finally, make sure they understand the directions for the activity by either restating them or asking students to restate them.

- For some students, the problem with writing is not that they can't think of anything to say; rather, they think of *too many* things to say. When this happens, they may be able to write a topic sentence, but their supporting sentences may be unrelated to the main topic or be repetitive. For these students, take a step-by-step approach. Every time they start to write a supporting sentence, ask them to first reread the topic sentence and then ask themselves, "Does this sentence relate to the topic?" If the answer is *yes*, they should add the sentence to the paragraph. If the answer is *no*, they shouldn't write the sentence.

FIGURE 4.26.1 : Topic Sentence Development

1. A paragraph is a group of sentences that all relate to a single topic.

2. A topic is expressed in one sentence, which unifies all of the other sentences in the paragraph.

3. A topic sentence is usually the first sentence in a paragraph. It should not be too narrow or too broad; instead, it should include only the most important idea.

What one sentence captures the topic of your paragraph? This is your topic sentence:

Your topic sentence should unify the supporting sentences in the same paragraph.

What is a detail about your topic that can be developed into a sentence?

What is a detail about your topic that can be developed into a sentence?

What is a detail about your topic that can be developed into a sentence?

What is a detail about your topic that can be developed into a sentence?

All of these sentences should relate to your topic sentence.

Strategy 27: Transitions Book and Transitions Bingo

Transition words and phrases are essential to written compositions because they hold ideas together and make for a smoother reading experience. Using transition words effectively affects coherence, organization, and word choice, and it helps students develop their ideas. Writers who do not use transitions (or who use them incorrectly) often end up with compositions that are disconnected, making them difficult for readers to understand. Even the best writers can have trouble recalling some transition words and phrases. Therefore, it's helpful to teach students how to create their own reference guides in order to use transitions effectively.

1. Make two-sided copies of the Transitions Book (Figure 4.27.1) for each student. Have students fold along the dotted lines and cut where indicated. The booklet should be folded so the page numbers are sequenced correctly. Staple the spine.
2. Make a teacher copy of the transitions book, and project it during instruction.
3. Explain that transitions are words or phrases that hold ideas together by bridging sentences and paragraphs to one another. Review example words and phrases (Figure 4.27.2), and then ask students to provide their own examples as a way to check for understanding.
4. Explain to students that they should use their Transitions Books as a reference guide whenever they work on compositions. We have intentionally left some room in the booklet for students to add their own transition words.

As an activity to reinforce the correct use of transitions, play a game of Transitions Bingo:

1. Hand out a Transitions Bingo card (Figure 4.27.3) to each student, and identify five groups/types of transitions to include in the header row. These will be the "topics" of the five columns.
2. Make sure you have a master list of all of the transition words generated by you and your students. Tell students which categories to write at the top of each column.
3. Review with students until you feel they are comfortable enough with transition words to play the game successfully.
4. Ask students to complete their bingo cards by writing a transition word or phrase (from their Transition Books or their memories) in each box. Remind them that the words and phrases they write should be appropriate for the heading of each column.

5. After students have completed their cards, begin calling out transition words and phrases at random from your master list.

6. The first student to cross out five words or phrases in a row—vertically, horizontally, or diagonally—wins. Repeat this game often to review transitions.

 Tip

Have some completed copies of the Transitions Book available for students who forget or lose theirs. This way, students can have the book for reference without falling behind.

 Alternatives and Accommodations

- When students have not regularly used transition words or phrases in their writing, you may need to add a step to your instruction. After introducing the words and phrases in Figure 4.27.2, provide students with written passages and ask them to highlight all the transitions they can find.

- One way to help students who are well below grade level and struggling with reading and writing is to provide them with a completed Transitions Book that has basic transition words and phrases already included. Ask students to add new transition words and phrases as they learn them so they begin to "take over" the process on their own.

- When playing the bingo game, fill in some of the boxes ahead of time. This provides students with examples and keeps them motivated when they struggle to understand.

FIGURE 4.27.1 : Transitions Book

Transitions to Summarize

As a result

Thus

In short

My Little Book of
Transitions

Transitions are like bridges helping
to connect sentences and paragraphs
from one to the next.

Transitions to Use to
Add Information

Again

Besides

Fold

8

1

Transitions to Repeat

Transitions to Compare

Similarly

Transitions to Contrast

But

Conversely

Fold

6

3

Transitions to Emphasize a Point

For this reason

Indeed

Transitions to Show Time

Transitions to Show Locations

Fold

2

7

Transitions to Show Sequence

Transitions to Give an Example

Fold

4

5

FIGURE 4.27.2 : Transition Words and Phrases

Transitions that add information	Transitions that emphasize a point	Transitions that compare	Transitions that contrast
additionally	always	accordingly	after all
again	another key point	also	although
besides	for this reason	as	but
finally	frequently	by comparison	by contrast
for example	important to remember	compared to	conversely
further	indeed	just as	even so
furthermore	in fact	like	however
likewise	most compelling	likewise	in contrast to
in addition	most importantly	in conjunction	meanwhile
moreover	obviously	in the same manner	nevertheless
next	on the negative/positive side	similarly	on the contrary
too	surprisingly	sometimes	on the other hand
what's more			otherwise
			whereas
			yet

Transitions that show sequence	Transitions that clarify	Transitions that repeat	Transitions that show time
after	for example	as aforementioned	finally
afterward	for instance	as aforesaid	formerly
at this time	in another case	as noted	immediately
before this	in other words	in brief	later
concurrently	in this situation		next
consequently	to clarify		previously
first	to demonstrate		soon
following this	to illustrate		then
hence	that is		thereafter
next			
now			
previously			
second			
soon			
subsequently			
then			
therefore			
third			
thus			

FIGURE 4.27.3 : Transitions Bingo Card

1. Your teacher will choose five transition groups/types. Write these transition types at the top of each column.

2. Complete the bingo card by writing an appropriate transition word or phrase (from your Transitions Book or memory) in each box.

3. Listen carefully as your teacher calls out transition words and phrases. If you hear a word or phrase that you also have on your bingo card, cross it out or place an *X* in that square.

4. When you cross out five words or phrases in a row—vertically, horizontally, or diagonally—call out, "Bingo!" The first student to do so wins the game!

Transitions that	Transitions that	Transitions that	Transitions that	Transitions that

Strategy 28: Transitions Spinner

Compositions need transition words and phrases to connect ideas, sentences, and paragraphs to one another. To help students develop the habit of using transitions in their writing, consider using the Transitions Spinner for a range of fun activities.

1. Copy the Transitions Spinner (Figure 4.28.1) on heavy paper and laminate it. You can buy a spinner arrow at a teacher supply store or make your own with a large paper clip. The eight categories are transitions that show time (e.g., *first, then*), repeat (e.g., *as mentioned above, in brief*), clarify (e.g., *for example, in other words*), show sequence (e.g., *after, at this time*), compare (e.g., *compared to, likewise*), contrast (e.g., *although, even so*), emphasize a point (e.g., *obviously, frequently*), and add information (e.g., *in addition, too*).

2. If students have already made Transitions Books (see Strategy 27), allow them to refer to it as they play this game.

3. Flick the spinner and call out the transitions category it lands on. Students can then do one of the following:

   • Locate transition words and phrases from the respective category in an essay you have copied and distributed. (If you play with this option, make sure you have given a copy of the essay to each student and provided an opportunity for them to read through it before beginning to play.) The first student to call out an answer gets a point. The student or team with the most points at the end wins the game. Before beginning the game, set the rules (including any time limits), indicate point goals, and explain whether students can repeat words or phrases.

   • Locate or write transitions in their own compositions. If you use this approach, make sure each student has selected a composition with enough transition words or phrases to take several turns. If not, allow students to play with partners or in small groups.

   • Announce a transition word or phrase that belongs in the respective category. This is a good option to use while introducing the concept of transitions and how to use them effectively.

Tip

Before beginning this strategy, show students the different categories and explain what each means. Then give students a list of transition words and phrases and ask them to put each in the correct category.

Alternatives and Accommodations

- The transitions spinner can be created with fewer categories so students can focus on key transitions first. This may also help students who are having difficulty grasping the concept.

- If students are having difficulty reading, play the game according to the rules of the first option described above but provide students with reading passages at two separate reading levels. Students do not need to know which level they have been assigned. If the passages share some common transition words and phrases, then all students can participate without embarrassment and it will be meaningful to everyone.

- Allow students to highlight transition words and phrases in their assigned essays before beginning the game. Students are then familiar with the transitions and are ready to play.

FIGURE 4.28.1 : Transitions Spinner

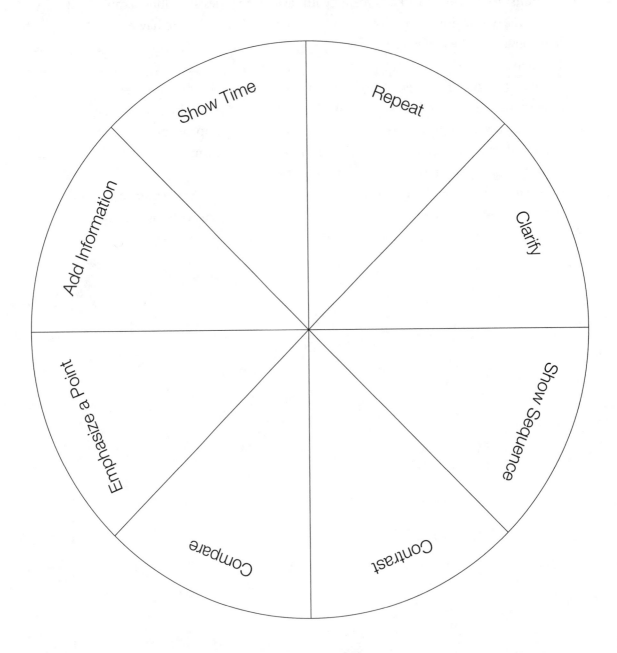

Strategy 29: Vocabulary Line-Up

When students use the right words in their writing, they clarify ideas and create strong images that enlighten the reader. Quite often, though, their word choice is limited. They use simple and repetitive words such as *said, it, very, really,* and *one* (e.g., *one day . . ., one morning . . ., one time . . .*). In this strategy, students note how established, professional writers use words to create meaning. Then they create a glossary of their own (organized by part of speech), which they can refer to as they write. Students also make a glossary of academic language they can use in their writing.

1. Make and distribute copies of the vertical strips (Figure 4.29.1). Begin with at least four strips per student, and add more later.

2. Ask students to write one of the following parts of speech at the top of each strip: adverbs, verbs, nouns, or adjectives.

3. Choose an on-level essay or passage, and instruct students to identify words or phrases they have never used (or don't usually use) in their own writing, would like to use in their own writing, or believe enlighten the reader.

4. Have students write these words on the respective strips. (A completed example is provided in Figure 4.29.2.) If students do not know the part of speech, have them look up the word in the dictionary.

5. After students write their words on the strips, use a brad fastener or ring to bind these together. They can continue to add more strips as they read other passages and encounter other words.

6. Ask students to commit to using at least three new words on their next writing assignments.

 ## Tip

This strategy is easily customizable for any number of grammatical structures, such as prepositional phrases, transition words, academic language, and figurative language (e.g., similes and metaphors).

 ## Alternatives and Accommodations

- Students who are learning to read and write in English may have long lists of words they have never used before. Although they may be familiar with the equivalent words in their native language, they may not use the English words frequently enough to feel confident and include them in their writing. To help them make this transition, allow English language learners to write a translated word beneath or beside each English word. This may help them use the new words more often in their writing.

- For students whose reading levels might make this activity more of a challenge, highlight challenging words in the passage before they begin to read. Ask students to tell you some definitions so you can help them assign the words to categories. Review (or teach) the meaning of unfamiliar words, and use each word in a simple sentence. This way, when students read the passage, they will have at least a basic amount of prior knowledge.

- For students who cannot reliably assign words to a part of speech (i.e., they don't know if a word is a noun or a verb), write a definition at the top of each list and provide one or two examples. Having some examples to refer to should help students remember the parts of speech and categorize words correctly.

FIGURE 4.29.1 : Vocabulary Line-Up

⭘	⭘	⭘	⭘
_____I've never used before	_____I've never used before	_____I've never used before	_____I've never used before

FIGURE 4.29.2 : Vocabulary Line-Up Example

Nouns I've never used before.	Adjectives I've never used before.	Verbs I've never used before.	Adverbs I've never used before.
image	magnificent	afford	literally
host	well-made	attempt	willfully
businessperson	elongated	command	delicately
sales clerk			brutally

Strategy 30: Word Stars

Although some student writers struggle to find the right words, others simply do not know that using words repeatedly leaves their passages dull and inconsequential. One way to help students use words that enliven their writing is to teach them how a thesaurus can provide them with new words that share meanings or have similar connotations but have distinct significance. Word stars are an excellent way to help students choose varying words that can clarify their writing.

1. Make sure each student has a thesaurus. Discuss key features of a thesaurus, such as synonyms, autonyms, and parts of speech. Ask students to use the thesaurus to practice generating synonyms for vocabulary words that you read aloud. As students suggest synonyms, discuss the similarities and differences among the words. Make sure that students understand that even though words are synonyms, they are not necessarily interchangeable. Point out that they should not use words they do not understand.

2. Distribute copies of the word stars (Figure 4.30.1), and have students cut them out.

3. Have them write a word they frequently use in the center of the star.

4. Then have students find synonyms and other related words in a thesaurus and write one on each point of the star.

5. Remind students to use some of these new words in their writing to replace the word they wrote in the center of the star.

 ## Tip

Clip the stars together with a ring binder, and have students continue to add to their collection throughout the year. They can refer to their collection whenever they have a writing assignment. Have students share their stars with classmates who struggle to find the precise word.

 ## Alternatives and Accommodations

- Students who are learning English can make bilingual word stars. They can include the English words along with the words in their native language. The easiest way for them to do this would be to put English on one side of the star and the other language on the opposite side. This approach can not only help them improve their writing vocabulary but also increase their proficiency in spoken English.

- If students are struggling with reading, allow them to create their own dictionaries or thesauri. In addition to the words and their associated definitions and synonyms, ask students to illustrate their books. Illustrations will help them remember the word meanings as they write.

- If students have difficulty, assign them a partner and allow them to take turns. Students can alternate suggesting synonyms. This will provide exposure to the words and set an expectation for them to complete the assignment, even though it may be difficult for them.

FIGURE 4.30.1 : Word Stars

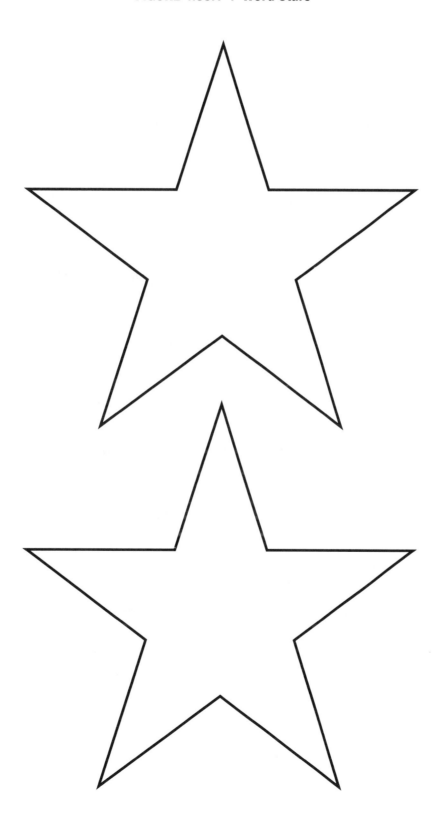

5

Tools for Convention and Presentation

The materials in this chapter are designed to reinforce concepts and rules associated with convention and presentation. We've included two sets of materials: those that can be used for instruction (i.e., they can be photocopied and provided to each student, or they can be projected for the entire class to see) and those that can be used by students as they work to produce a final piece of writing.

Tools to Augment Instruction on Capitalization

To remember three important rules for capitalization, teach students to think of the mnemonic device BPS. *B* represents beginning, *P* represents proper, and *S* represents specific names. Below are some examples to help students better understand BPS. After reviewing the rules, students can use the BPS Checklist (Figure 5.1, page 174) to help them use capital letters correctly in their sentences, paragraphs, and essays.

Capitalization Rules

First word of a sentence	• <u>H</u>e needed to get his eyes checked.
	• <u>I</u>t had been two years since his last checkup.
	• <u>H</u>is mother made an appointment for him to see the eye doctor.

Proper nouns (nouns that name a person, place, or thing)	• <u>M</u>ichael got a new pair of glasses. • He visited <u>L</u>enscrafters after his visit to <u>D</u>r. <u>B</u>abcock's office. • He was disappointed that he couldn't buy the newest pair of <u>O</u>akley frames.
Specific names	• <u>M</u>other <u>T</u>eresa did a lot of good during her life. • <u>A</u>braham <u>L</u>incoln is considered to be one of the best presidents. • <u>T</u>oo <u>T</u>all <u>J</u>ones was a football player.
Cities and states	• I live in <u>A</u>ustin, <u>T</u>exas.
Languages	• I speak <u>E</u>nglish and <u>S</u>panish.
Countries and nationalities	• Kevin and Ben are <u>N</u>orwegian businessmen who met in <u>M</u>exico.
Days of the week	• Can you spend the night on <u>F</u>riday so we can shop together on <u>S</u>aturday?
Months of the year	• I'll be on vacation in <u>J</u>une, but I'll be back at school in <u>A</u>ugust.
Planets	• I wish I could travel through space to see <u>M</u>ars and <u>S</u>aturn.
Religions and holidays	• My mother is <u>C</u>atholic, and my father is <u>M</u>uslim. • We celebrate both <u>C</u>hristmas and <u>R</u>amadan. • We never celebrate <u>H</u>alloween.
Name brands	• I love <u>O</u>reo cookies and <u>H</u>ershey chocolates.
Titles of books, articles, songs, poems, movies, etc. (do not capitalize preposition or articles unless these words begin the title)	• The library has *Time* and *Newsweek*. • Did you read the article "<u>J</u>unk <u>F</u>ood on the <u>R</u>ise"? • My favorite book is *<u>T</u>he <u>H</u>igh <u>T</u>ide*. • We should see the movie *<u>G</u>reen <u>E</u>merald*.

FIGURE 5.1 : BPS Checklist

Name:_____ Date:_____

Essay Title:_____

My Capitalization Checklist	Yes	No	N/A
B I capitalized the word at the **beginning** of each sentence.	☐	☐	☐
P I capitalized all **proper** nouns.	☐	☐	☐
S I capitalized all words that are **specific** names.	☐	☐	☐

Peer Editor's Capitalization Checklist	Yes	No	N/A
B He/She capitalized the word at the **beginning** of each sentence.	☐	☐	☐
P He/She capitalized all **proper** nouns.	☐	☐	☐
S He/She capitalized all words that are **specific** names.	☐	☐	☐

Teacher's Capitalization Checklist	Yes	No	N/A
B The **beginning** of each sentence is capitalized correctly.	☐	☐	☐
P All **proper** nouns are capitalized correctly.	☐	☐	☐
S All words that are **specific** people, places, and things are capitalized correctly.	☐	☐	☐

Comments:

Tools to Augment Instruction on Comma Usage

There are many rules to keep in mind when you use a comma. Below are some basic rules with examples to help students understand the comma better. After reviewing the rules, use the Comma Usage Checklist (Figure 5.2, page 176) to help them use commas correctly in their sentences, paragraphs, and essays.

Comma Usage Rules

When you have several words in a series or list	• Bananas, peaches, and plums are my favorite fruit. • I visited Chicago, New York, and Los Angeles this summer. • I'm pretty good at jumping rope, jogging, and biking. • My grandma is sweet, kind, and affectionate.
Between a month/day and the year in dates	• She was born August 22, 1996. • We will never forget September 11, 2001.
After the year when a month/day and year are used	• They were engaged on July 1, 1970, and wed later that year. • February 21, 1990, was the day my parents bought our house.
Between a city and a state	• Walt Disney World is in Orlando, Florida. • Harvard University is in Cambridge, Massachusetts. • The conference was held in Denver, Colorado.
Between a city and a country	• Ericka just came back from Rome, Italy. • The movie was filmed in Tokyo, Japan.
After a country when used with a city	• She would rather visit Paris, France, than London, England. • I would love to travel to Dublin, Ireland, in the summer. • We spent the holiday in Santiago, Chile, before coming home.

FIGURE 5.2 : Comma Usage Checklist

Name: _____ Date: _____

Essay Title: _____

My Comma Usage Checklist	Yes	No	N/A
I used commas when I had several words in a series or list.	☐	☐	☐
I used commas when I used a month/day and the year in dates.	☐	☐	☐
I used a comma after the year when a month/day and year are used.	☐	☐	☐
I used a comma between a city and a state.	☐	☐	☐
I used a comma between a city and a country.	☐	☐	☐
I used a comma after a country when used with a city.	☐	☐	☐

Peer Editor's Comma Usage Checklist	Yes	No	N/A
He/She used commas when there were several items in a series or list.	☐	☐	☐
He/She used commas between a month/day and the year in dates.	☐	☐	☐
He/She used a comma after the year when a month/day and year are used.	☐	☐	☐
He/She used a comma between a city and a state.	☐	☐	☐
He/She used a comma between a city and a country.	☐	☐	☐
He/She used a comma after a country when used with a city.	☐	☐	☐

Teacher's Comma Usage Checklist	Yes	No	N/A
The student used commas when there were several items in a series or list.	☐	☐	☐
The student used commas between a month/day and the year in dates.	☐	☐	☐
The student used commas after the year when a month/day and year are used.	☐	☐	☐
The student used a comma between a city and a state.	☐	☐	☐
The student used a comma between a city and a country.	☐	☐	☐
The student used a comma after a country when used with a city.	☐	☐	☐

Tools to Augment Instruction on Apostrophe Usage

There are many rules to keep in mind when you use an apostrophe. Below are some basic rules with examples to help students understand the apostrophe better. After reviewing the rules, use the Apostrophe Usage Checklist (Figure 5.3, page 180) to help them use apostrophes correctly in their sentences, paragraphs, and essays.

Apostrophe Usage Rules

When you have a contraction of two words, use an apostrophe to replace the missing letter(s).	
am, are, is	he is → he's I am → I'm it is → it's she is → she's they are → they're we are → we're you are → you're
had	he had → he'd I had → I'd it had → it'd she had → she'd they had → they'd we had → we'd you had → you'd
has, have	he has → he's I have → I've must have → must've she has → she's should have → should've they have → they've we have → we've would have → would've you have → you've
is	here is → here's there is → there's what is → what's where is → where's

not	are not → aren't could not → couldn't did not → didn't do not → don't does not → doesn't had not → hadn't has not → hasn't have not → haven't is not → isn't must not → mustn't should not → shouldn't will not → won't would not → wouldn't
us	let us → let's
will	he will → he'll I will → I'll it will → it'll she will → she'll they will → they'll we will → we'll you will → you'll
would	he would → he'd I would → I'd it would → it'd she would → she'd they would → they'd we would → we'd you would → you'd

Some Important Notes:

- The contraction for *can not* can be written as either *cannot* or *can't*.
- There are contractions for *it would* and *it had* (i.e., *it'd*), but because they are rarely used, it's best to keep the two words separate.
- The contractions for *must have* and *should have* are always *must've* and *should've*. A common mistake is writing *must of* and *should of*.
- Do not confuse the contraction *they're* with *their* (i.e., plural possessive pronoun that is used before a noun, such as *their* car, *their* friends, *their* lawnmower, etc.) and *there*.
- *It's* is a contraction for *it is*. The possessive pronoun *its* (e.g., The dog chases *its* tail) has no apostrophe.

Use an apostrophe with singular and plural possessives.	
singular possessive (apostrophe + *s* is added to the end of the singular noun)	• Simon's friend lives in California. • That cat's tail is long. • Connie complimented Alex's haircut. • The phone's case is durable. • James's house is really big!
plural possessive: for nouns that end in *s* (apostrophe is added to the end of the plural noun)	• The two fathers' watches were similar. • Nine banks' interest rates were competitively low. • Several of the cars' windshields were damaged in the storm. • All of the players' shoes are muddy. • Both of the lamps' shades are dusty.
plural possessive: for irregular nouns that don't end in *s* (apostrophe + *s* is added to the end of the plural noun)	• Larry asked where the men's suits were located. • The women's sandals are on sale. • We played with the children's toys. • The deer's hoofs made a loud noise on the deck. • The mayor knew the people's intentions.

FIGURE 5.3 : Apostrophe Usage Checklist

Name: _____ Date: _____

Essay Title: _____

My Apostrophe Usage Checklist	Yes	No	N/A
I used an apostrophe when I contracted two words.	☐	☐	☐
I used an apostrophe where letters were omitted.	☐	☐	☐
I used an apostrophe + *s* with singular possessive nouns (i.e., *'s*).	☐	☐	☐
I used an apostrophe with plural possessive nouns that end in *s* (i.e., *s'*).	☐	☐	☐
I used an apostrophe + *s* with plural nouns that don't end in *s* (i.e., *'s*).	☐	☐	☐

Peer Editor's Apostrophe Usage Checklist	Yes	No	N/A
He/She used an apostrophe to contract two words.	☐	☐	☐
He/She used an apostrophe where letters were omitted.	☐	☐	☐
He/She used an apostrophe + *s* with singular possessive nouns (i.e., *'s*).	☐	☐	☐
He/She used an apostrophe with plural possessive nouns that end in *s* (i.e., *s'*).	☐	☐	☐
He/She used an apostrophe + *s* with plural nouns that don't end in *s* (i.e., *'s*).	☐	☐	☐

Teacher's Apostrophe Usage Checklist	Yes	No	N/A
The student used an apostrophe to contract two words.	☐	☐	☐
The student used an apostrophe where letters were omitted.	☐	☐	☐
The student used an apostrophe + *s* with singular possessive nouns (i.e., *'s*).	☐	☐	☐
The student used an apostrophe with plural possessive nouns that end in *s* (i.e., *s'*).	☐	☐	☐
The student used an apostrophe + *s* with plural nouns that don't end in *s* (i.e., *'s*).	☐	☐	☐

Tools to Augment Instruction on Colons and Semicolons

There are many rules to keep in mind when you use colons and semicolons. Below are some basic rules with examples to help students understand the colon and semicolon better. After reviewing the rules, students cans use the Colon and Semicolon Usage Checklist (Figure 5.4, page 184) to help them use colons and semicolons correctly in their sentences, paragraphs, and essays.

Colon Usage Rules

After a complete sentence (independent clause) that introduces a list	• Javier has many talents: dancing, singing, and acting. • Keisha told everyone her birthday wishes: to have a small party, a chocolate cake, and plenty of gifts. • I want a clean kitchen when I return: swept and mopped floors, dishes put away, and clean counters.
Some Important Notes! Do not use a colon if you are using the words *include, includes, including, for, for example, that is,* or *namely.*	• **Incorrect:** I'm going to invite all of my friends to the party, including: Jonah, Ralph, Renea, and Tamika. • **Correct:** I'm going to invite all of my friends to the party, including Jonah, Ralph, Renea, and Tamika. • **Incorrect:** She baked a cake for: the neighbor, the mail carrier, and the gardener. • **Correct:** She baked a cake for the neighbor, the mail carrier, and the gardener.

Do not use a colon if there isn't an independent clause introducing the list.	• **Incorrect:** Charles thought we should: drive to Connecticut, Massachusetts, and New Hampshire. • **Correct:** Charles thought we should drive to Connecticut, Massachusetts, and New Hampshire. • **Incorrect:** The newspaper: print was too small; the margins were too wide; and the titles were offset. • **Correct:** The newspaper print was too small; the margins were too wide; and the titles were offset.
After a complete sentence (independent clause) that introduces a direct quote	• They shouted with glee: "We are victorious!" • Candace shocked everyone with her intention: "I'm still going to marry him." • In his own words, he expressed that the car was a lemon: "No one can fix that piece of junk."
After a complete sentence (independent clause) that introduces an appositive	• We finally bought the perfect car for us: a convertible. • Sheila looked high and low for the most comfortable slippers: moccasins. • Tim knew who gave him the most support: his children.
After a complete sentence (independent clause) that introduces another closely related independent clause that clarifies the first	• That is one fine suit: the craftsmanship is impeccable. • The tamales were tasty: each one packed with flavor. • The professor is inspiring: no one ever misses his lectures.

Used to separate a title and subtitle	• The book *Grammar in Action: Daily Tools for Everyone* was useful. • For my birthday, Shelly gave me *The Eagle Has Strength: So Do You.* • Chuy was busy reading *Excellence at Work: A Journey to Triumph.*
Used in the salutation line of a business letter	• Dear Mr. President: • To Whom It May Concern: • Dear Consumer Affairs:

Semicolon Usage Rules

Connects two complete sentences (independent clauses) without using *and, but, or, nor, for, so,* or *yet* (Generally, the two clauses are related to or contrast each other.)	• Crystal gave her presentation in 15 minutes; Dr. Marion called on Nannette to go next. • Our dentist came to the party; he told jokes all night long. • The hikers made their plans at the restaurant; they bought their supplies at the store next door.
Separates items in a list that contains commas for dates, geographic locations, or descriptions	• My children's birthdays are July 3, 2000; August 22, 2004; and January 20, 2008. • Ignacio's favorite cities include Marble Falls, Texas; Fort Wayne, Indiana; and Edgartown, Massachusetts. • Before the remodel, the carpet was stained; the window was broken; and none of the plugs worked.

FIGURE 5.4 : Colon and Semicolon Usage Checklist

Name:_____ Date:_____

Essay Title:_____

My Colon and Semicolon Usage Checklist	Yes	No	N/A
I used a colon after a complete sentence that introduced a list.	☐	☐	☐
I used a colon after a complete sentence that introduced a direct quote.	☐	☐	☐
I used a colon after a complete sentence that introduced an appositive.	☐	☐	☐
I used a colon after a complete sentence that introduced another closely related independent clause that clarifies the first.	☐	☐	☐
I used a colon to separate a title and subtitle.	☐	☐	☐
I used a colon in the salutation line of a business letter.	☐	☐	☐
I used a semicolon to connect two complete sentences without using *and*, *but*, *or*, *nor*, *for*, *so*, or *yet*.	☐	☐	☐
I used a semicolon to connect two complete sentences that have internal punctuation, such as commas.	☐	☐	☐
I used a semicolon to separate items in a list that contains commas for dates, geographic locations, and descriptions.	☐	☐	☐

Peer Editor's Colon and Semicolon Usage Checklist	Yes	No	N/A
He/She used a colon after a complete sentence that introduced a list.	☐	☐	☐
He/She used a colon after a complete sentence that introduced a direct quote.	☐	☐	☐
He/She used a colon after a complete sentence that introduced an appositive.	☐	☐	☐
He/She used a colon after a complete sentence that introduced another closely related independent clause that clarifies the first.	☐	☐	☐
He/She used a colon to separate a title and subtitle.	☐	☐	☐
He/She used a colon in the salutation line of a business letter.	☐	☐	☐
He/She used a semicolon to connect two complete sentences without using *and*, *but*, *or*, *nor*, *for*, *so*, or *yet*.	☐	☐	☐
He/She used a semicolon to connect two complete sentences that have internal punctuation, such as commas.	☐	☐	☐
He/She used a semicolon to separate items in a list that contains commas for dates, geographic locations, and descriptions.	☐	☐	☐

Teacher's Colon and Semicolon Usage Checklist	Yes	No	N/A
The student used a colon after a complete sentence that introduced a list.	☐	☐	☐
The student used a colon after a complete sentence that introduced a direct quote.	☐	☐	☐
The student used a colon after a complete sentence that introduced an appositive.	☐	☐	☐
The student used a colon after a complete sentence that introduced another closely related independent clause that clarifies the first.	☐	☐	☐
The student used a colon to separate a title and subtitle.	☐	☐	☐
The student used a colon in the salutation line of a business letter.	☐	☐	☐
The student used a semicolon to connect two complete sentences without using *and*, *but*, *or*, *nor*, *for*, *so*, or *yet*.	☐	☐	☐
The student used a semicolon to connect two complete sentences that have internal punctuation, such as commas.	☐	☐	☐
The student used a semicolon to separate items in a list that contains commas for dates, geographic locations, and descriptions.	☐	☐	☐

Tools to Augment Instruction on Common Spelling Errors

Below are some basic rules with examples that can help students become a better speller.

Commonly Misspelled Words

Word	Example Sentence	Note
already	I was <u>already</u> home when I got the phone call.	Never write *allready*.
alright	Bruce decided it was <u>alright</u> for his daughter to spend the night.	Never write *allright*.
choose	Tamika will <u>choose</u> what to wear in the morning.	This word means "to decide" or "to select."
chose	Emilio <u>chose</u> to go first.	This word is the past tense of *choose*.
defi-nitely	The dogs <u>definitely</u> need a walk.	Never write *definately*.
embar-rass	The main character plans to <u>embarrass</u> her enemy.	Note the double *r* and the double *s*.
its	<u>Its</u> hind legs and paws were scraped.	This word is a possessive pronoun. No apostrophe is used.
it's	<u>It's</u> amazing that we've had so much rain.	This word is the contraction for *it is*.
lose	I hope my team doesn't <u>lose</u> the game.	This word means "to come to be without" or "fail to maintain."
loose	Michelle's jeans fit her <u>loose</u>.	This word means "to be free from binding or restraint."
separate	They sat <u>separate</u> from one another.	There is "a rat" in separate.
than	Fernando ate more <u>than</u> usual.	This word is used to compare.
then	Regina plans to move and <u>then</u> buy a car.	This word is used in the order of time.

Word	Example Sentence	Note
their	<u>Their</u> Internet connection is slow.	This word is the possessive form of *they*.
there	<u>There</u> were so many leaves on the playground.	This word means "at a place," "at that point," etc.
they're	<u>They're</u> about to leave for San Francisco.	This word is the contraction for *they are*.
your	When is <u>your</u> cousin coming to visit?	This word is the possessive form of *you*.
you're	<u>You're</u> about to receive some wonderful news.	This word is the contraction for *you are*.

Spelling Rules

From our experiences, students have struggled with the following spelling guidelines. Although this list certainly can be expanded upon, it should cover the basics.

For words that have the long *e* sound, use *i* before *e*, except after *c*.	achieve belief brief priest relieve	ceiling conceit deceive receive receipt
Exceptions to the above rule: some words have a long *e* sound but are spelled *ei*.		either leisure neither seize weird
For words that have the long *a* sound, use *e* before *i*.		neighbor reign veil weigh

For words with the prefixes *ante-*, *anti-*, *dis-*, *for-*, *fore-*, *mis-*, and *over-*, add the prefix to the original spelling of the root word.	*anti*biotic *anti*lock *anti*virus *ante*room *ante*chapel *dis*appear *dis*appoint *dis*continue *for*ever *for*given *for*saken	*fore*cast *fore*ground *fore*worn *mis*align *mis*interpret *mis*spoken *over*extended *over*rated *over*stated	
When a word ends with a consonant + *y*, change the *y* to *i* before adding a suffix (except for the suffix *-ing*, when you should keep the *y*).	apply bully cry dry marry party study supply	applied bullied cried dried married partied studied supplied	applying bullying crying drying marrying partying studying supplying
When a noun ends with a consonant + *y* and you want to make it plural, change the *y* to *i* and add *es*.	ally baby battery company puppy	allies babies batteries companies puppies	
For words that do not end in *y*, the spelling of the word stays the same when adding the suffixes *-ly* and *-ness*.	calm cheerful hopeful abusive bitter like	calmly cheerfully hopefully abusiveness bitterness likeness	

For words that end in *y*, change the final *y* to *i* before adding the suffixes *-ly* and *-ness*.	heavy hungry necessary blurry clumsy crazy	heavily hungrily necessarily blurriness clumsiness craziness
For words that end in *e*, the spelling of the word stays the same when adding a suffix that begins with a consonant (e.g., *-ful, -ment, -less, -ly*). (Note that some exceptions exist, such as *argue* and *acknowledge: argument* and *acknowledgment*.)	advise fate hate intense use	advisement fateful hateful intensely useless
For words that end in *e*, drop the *e* before adding a suffix that begins with a vowel (e.g., *-ing*).	bike devise give hope solve	biking devising giving hoping solving

Tools for Presentation

So that students' paragraphs and essays have a neat appearance, keep in mind the following general rules. Have them use the Presentation Checklist (Figure 5.5, page 190) to develop a paragraph or essay that has good presentation. Pieces of writing with good presentation have

- A heading.
- A title.
- Margins that are an appropriate size. (Most papers have a one-inch margin on all four sides.)
- Few or no smears or eraser marks.
- Few or no deletion and insertion marks.
- Appropriate and complementary graphics.

FIGURE 5.5 : Presentation Checklist

Name: _____ Date: _____

Essay Title: _____

My Presentation Checklist	Yes	No	N/A
I used headings.	☐	☐	☐
I included a title.	☐	☐	☐
My margins are an appropriate size.	☐	☐	☐
There are few (or no) smears or eraser marks on my paper.	☐	☐	☐
There are few (or no) deletion or insertion marks on my paper.	☐	☐	☐
I used appropriate and complementary graphics.	☐	☐	☐

Peer Editor's Presentation Checklist	Yes	No	N/A
He/She used headings.	☐	☐	☐
He/She included a title.	☐	☐	☐
His/Her margins are an appropriate size.	☐	☐	☐
There are few (or no) smears or eraser marks on his/her paper.	☐	☐	☐
There are few (or no) deletion or insertion marks on his/her paper.	☐	☐	☐
He/She used appropriate and complementary graphics.	☐	☐	☐

Teacher's Presentation Checklist	Yes	No	N/A
The student used headings.	☐	☐	☐
The student included a title.	☐	☐	☐
The student's margins are an appropriate size.	☐	☐	☐
There are few (or no) smears or eraser marks on the student's paper.	☐	☐	☐
There are few (or no) deletion or insertion marks on the student's paper.	☐	☐	☐
The student used appropriate and complementary graphics.	☐	☐	☐

APPENDIXES

APPENDIX A

WRITING PROMPTS

Included here are various writing prompts, which include six illustrations that can be used for the pre- and post-test measures on the Evaluation Protocol.

For grades 3–5, consider these three illustrations and prompts:

The boy in the picture is going on an unexpected trip with his father, who happens to be a creative scientist. The father told the boy to pack light and prepare for an adventurous trip in his machine. Where are they going? Why? Write a story about what happens to the boy and his father.

The girls in the picture have come up with a recipe for a delicious drink that has great benefits. What are those benefits? Write about how the girls discovered the recipe, and describe the benefits to those who drink it.

The boy in the picture was reading his social studies textbook when Benjamin Franklin, Abraham Lincoln, and Martin Luther King, Jr., appeared in front of him. Write a story about why these famous figures from history decided to visit the boy and what he plans to do with them.

Source: Copyright 2014 David Campos and Kathleen Fad. Used with permission.

Some additional writing prompts include the following:

- Tell about a day when something wonderful happened to you. When you write your story, tell things in order and include details about that day.
- If someone gave you a camera and asked you to take pictures of three things or people that are special to you, what would you take pictures of? Explain why.
- Imagine that you are given the opportunity to travel to another country and you can pick where you would like to go. Where would you go and why?
- Students in your school district have not been doing very well, so the leaders of your school district are considering adding another half hour onto the end of the school day. Argue for or against this change, using arguments that will convince others that your position is the best one.
- Tell one thing that you have accomplished that you are most proud of, but that many people do not know. Describe what you have done and explain why you have done it.

For grades 6–8, consider these three illustrations and prompts:

The girl in the picture is surprised. Why? Her friends, who are huddled around a cell phone, are reading a text. What does the text say? Is it about the girl or something that happened at school? Write a story about the girl, the text message, and what's about to happen, especially since their teacher is fast approaching.

Source: Copyright 2014 David Campos and Kathleen Fad. Used with permission.

The boy in the picture received a mysterious video game in the mail. He had never seen it before and has no idea who sent it to him. As he plays the game, he thinks it's the best video game ever made. Who sent the video game? Why? What is the game about? Write a story about what the boy plans to do with the game after he has played it for a while.

Source: Copyright 2014 David Campos and Kathleen Fad. Used with permission.

The girl in the picture was just asked by the president of the United States to create a new national holiday. Describe the girl's new holiday, her reasons for choosing that day, and the customs and traditions she expects people to associate with the holiday.

Some additional writing prompts include the following:

- Do you think that success in life is due more to working hard, being smart, or having a good attitude? Include examples in your response.
- Recycling is good for the environment and also saves money. Write an argument for why your school should begin or improve a recycling program. Provide details and examples in your writing.
- Many people still smoke cigarettes, even though they know the health risks associated with smoking. Do you think that people who smoke should pay more for health insurance because they engage in unhealthy behavior?

- If you could introduce your friends to one special person, who would that person be? Tell about your relationship with that person and why you would want your friends to meet him/her.
- Write an argument either in favor of or against doing away with all textbooks and replacing them with electronic devices.

Finally, consider using these prompts for students who need added information to take a position and support their opinion:

- In recent years, Congress has had to make significant financial cutbacks to government-funded programs to save the U.S. economy. One of the agencies that has received severe cutbacks has been the National Aeronautics and Space Administration (NASA). Some government representatives would like the NASA budget decreased by several hundred million dollars! Should our government drastically cut back on NASA's budget? Write an essay that explains why such cutbacks are necessary. Alternatively, explain why such cutbacks could negatively affect space exploration. Be sure to support your opinion with details and examples.
- Over the last three decades, the number of overweight children and youth has increased dramatically. Medical experts believe that this trend is largely caused by unhealthy eating and physical activity practices. In one state, lawmakers have proposed that schools grade students on their health status. So, students who are underweight or overweight would get a lower grade (such as a D or F), and students who are at the ideal weight would get a higher grade (such as an A or B). The lawmakers believe that with such a grade, school officials and parents can then help students achieve an ideal weight. Write an essay in favor or against such a proposal. Be sure to support your opinion with details and examples.
- Many elementary schools throughout the country have terminated their art and music programs to increase the amount of time students can devote to learning the primary subjects. Some school officials believe that this important because the additional time can help students earn improved scores on standardized tests that measure reading and math achievement. Write an essay in favor or against such a proposal. Be sure to support your opinion with details and examples.
- Some school districts have zero tolerance policies that enforce suspensions and expulsions on students who bring drugs and/or alcohol to school, or smoke or commit violence acts on campus. Any student who breaks the zero tolerance policy—even if it is the first offense and it was accident—is banned from the school setting. Some students support zero tolerance policies because they ensure a safe campus. Others believe that zero tolerance policies are unfair because some school administrators can misinterpret them. In one district, for instance, a kindergartner was suspended for bringing to school a pink

Hello Kitty© bubble maker that was in the shape of a gun. Write an essay in favor of or against such zero tolerance policies. Be sure to support your opinion with details and examples.

APPENDIX B

DIRECTIONS FOR ADMINISTERING THE WRITING PROMPTS

For 3rd to 5th Grade Students

1. Choose one of the writing prompts found in Appendix A.

2. Say,

"I need everyone's attention. I need complete silence. I want you to write about a prompt that I'm going to read to you.

"Your essay will help me teach you to become a better writer. I want you to think about all aspects of writing you have learned so far and apply them in your writing. Here's your chance to show me your creative ability and your knowledge of capitalization, punctuation, spelling, and grammar.

"Remember that a good story has a beginning, a middle, and an end. Don't forget to describe your characters, setting, and plot, and use details and examples to make your story more interesting. Additionally, write your essay using complete sentences.

"Take a few minutes to organize what you want to write about. Then begin writing. You will have 30 minutes to write your story. If you need more time, just let me know."

3. Project the writing prompt, read it, and ask students to begin writing.

4. After 30 minutes, say,

"Stop. It's OK if you aren't finished. You can turn in what you have. How many of you would like some more time, though? I can give you an extra 15 minutes."

5. Collect students' essays. Read each one, and use an Evaluation Protocol (Appendix C) to evaluate students' writing. The directions are found in Chapter 3 on pages 29–31.

For 6th to 8th Grade Students

1. Choose one of the writing prompts found in Appendix A.

2. Say,

"I need everyone's attention. I need complete silence. I want you to write about a prompt that I'm going to read to you. Your story will help me identify your writing strengths and any areas that you need to develop.

"I want you to think about all aspects of writing you have learned so far and apply them in your story. Here's your chance to show me your creative ability and your knowledge of capitalization, punctuation, spelling, and grammar.

"Remember that a good story has a beginning, a middle, and an end. Don't forget to describe your characters, setting, and plot, and use details and examples to make your story more interesting. Additionally, you should write your essay using complete sentences.

"Take a few minutes to organize what you want to write about. Then begin writing. You will have 30 minutes to write your story. If you need more time, just let me know."

3. Project the writing prompt, read it, and ask students to begin writing.

4. After 30 minutes, say,

"Stop. It's OK if you aren't finished. You can turn in what you have. However, how many of you would like some more time? I can give you an extra 15 minutes."

5. Collect students' essays. Read each one, and use an Evaluation Protocol (Appendix C) to evaluate students' writing. The directions are found in Chapter 3 on pages 29–31.

APPENDIX C

EVALUATION PROTOCOL

TOOLS FOR TEACHING WRITING: STRATEGIES AND INTERVENTIONS FOR DIVERSE LEARNERS IN GRADES 3–8

EVALUATION PROTOCOL

Name _____

Birth Date _____ Age _____

School _____ Grade _____

Rater(s) _____

Date of Pretest _____ Prompt _____
Amount of Time Student Spent Writing _____

Date of Posttest _____ Prompt _____
Amount of Time Student Spent Writing _____

The evaluation provided in this form is linked to 30 instructional strategies, which are designed to support students who struggle with writing. The strategies should be used to develop the writing traits described below. This evaluation form can be used to support the RTI process in Tier 1 (whole-group or individual instruction), Tier 2 (small-group or individual instruction in specific areas), or Tier 3 (individual support and instruction). This form is intended to measure student progress and guide teachers as they plan and deliver individualized instruction.

THE WRITING TRAITS

▶ **FOCUS**
Focus is the central idea or controlling theme of a piece of writing. It's also known as "sticking to the point." Student writers achieve clear focus when they know what they want to write and how they want to write about it.

▶ **COHERENCE**
Coherence refers to the connection of ideas that support the focus. Effective student writers order their ideas so that each sentence and paragraph logically connects to the controlling theme.

▶ **ORGANIZATION**
Organization is evident when the essay or story is written in a fashion that makes sense. In other words, ideas are linked logically from sentence to sentence and from paragraph to paragraph.

▶ **DEVELOPMENT OF IDEAS**
Writers deepen their readers' understanding of the work through ideas that reveal depth of thought and substance.

▶ **VOICE**
Voice is what makes a writer's style unique. Convictions and feelings are evident through the writer's choice of words.

▶ **WORD CHOICE**
A good writer uses rich and precise language in a functional way that enlightens and engages the reader. Strong word choice can expand and clarify ideas, create strong images that connect the reader to the writing, and guide the reader to a new understanding of the topic.

▶ **CONVENTIONS**
The term *conventions* refers to the mechanics of writing—spelling, punctuation, capitalization, grammar, usage, and paragraphing. Students who understand the conventions spell high-frequency words correctly; apply standard spelling strategies; apply structural aspects of phonemes, diphthongs, and so forth; and use punctuation and capitalization rules effectively.

▶ **PRESENTATION**
Presentation refers to the appearance of the essay in actual form, on paper.

PRE- AND POSTTEST MEASURES

DIRECTIONS

❶ Administer a pretest using a prompt from Appendix A. Read aloud the directions for test administration (Appendix B). Allow students a minimum of 30 minutes to write about the prompt.

❷ After collecting students' essays, read them carefully. Decide whether each student demonstrates mastery of the writing traits by placing a check mark in the *yes* or *no* column beside the appropriate item(s) under each trait.

❸ In the "Strategy" column, specific interventions are listed and can be selected to address each item designated with a *no*. As you design your language arts lesson plans, decide which strategies to implement.

❹ Conference with the student using the Student and Teacher Reflection Form (Appendix D). During the conference, review the student's essay, describe what the student data indicate about the writing, identify your concerns, and write a formative critique of the writing.

❺ After completing the selected strategies (over a three-month period), administer a posttest using a prompt from Appendix A. Read aloud the directions for test administration (Appendix B). Allow students a minimum of 30 minutes to write about the prompt.

❻ After collecting the students' essays, read them carefully. Decide whether each student demonstrates mastery of the writing traits, and place a check mark in the *yes* or *no* column beside the appropriate item(s) under each trait.

Pretest Date:					Posttest Date:		
Can the student . . .	Yes	No	If *no* was checked, refer to these strategies		Can the student . . .	Yes	No
Focus	Yes	No	Strategy	Start Date	Focus	Yes	No
1 Establish a central idea or theme about the topic?			11 Magnifying Glass		Establish a central idea or theme about the topic?		
			14 Prewriting Pyramid				
			15 Questions to Clarify				
			20 Soccer, Anyone?				
			24 Stick to the Point				
2 Write a well-developed topic sentence?			1 3-2-1		Write a well-developed topic sentence?		
			15 Questions to Clarify				
			26 Topic Sentence Development				
3 Include little irrelevant information?			2 Check Yourself		Include little irrelevant information?		
			4 Editing Irrelevant Info				
			24 Stick to the Point				
4 Write for a variety of purposes and audiences?			7 Give Acting a Shot		Write for a variety of purposes and audiences?		
			12 My Main Purpose				
			14 Prewriting Pyramid				
			24 Stick to the Point				

Coherence		Yes	No	Strategy	Start Date	Coherence	Yes	No
1	Group related sentences within paragraphs?			3 Color Coding		Group related sentences within paragraphs?		
				19 Sequence Cards				
				20 Soccer, Anyone?				
2	Group related ideas into separate paragraphs?			1 3-2-1		Group related ideas into separate paragraphs?		
				2 Check Yourself				
				6 Flying High				
				19 Sequence Cards				
3	Convey a consistent point of view through-out the written piece?			3 Color Coding		Convey a consistent point of view through-out the written piece?		
				22 Spin Your Point of View				
				25 Three Tab POV				
4	Add supporting details that align with the focus?			2 Check Yourself		Add supporting details that align with the focus?		
				8 Graphic Organizers				
				15 Questions to Clarify				
				19 Sequence Cards				
				20 Soccer Anyone?				
				27 Transitions Book				
Organization		Yes	No	Strategy	Start Date	Organization	Yes	No
1	Use effective prewrit-ing strategies, such as webs, timelines, or outlines?			6 Flying High		Use effective prewrit-ing strategies such as webs, timelines, or outlines?		
				8 Graphic Organizers				
				13 Plan It Out				
				14 Prewriting Pyramid				
				19 Sequence Cards				
				22 Spin Your Point of View				
				23 Split Voice				
2	Apply transitions to guide the reader through the written piece?			15 Questions to Clarify		Apply transitions to guide the reader through the written piece?		
				27 Transitions Book				
				28 Transition Spinner				
3	Organize writing in a logical sequence around a central idea?			6 Flying High		Organize writing in a logical sequence around a central idea?		
				8 Graphic Organizers				
				12 My Main Purpose				
				14 Prewriting Pyramid				
				19 Sequence Cards				
				20 Soccer, Anyone?				
4	Arrange ideas to con-vey meaning through the use of strategies, such as chronology, cause and effect, and compare and contrast?			8 Graphic Organizers		Arrange ideas to con-vey meaning through the use of strategies, such as chronology, cause and effect, and compare and contrast?		
				13 Plan It Out				
				27 Transitions Book				

Development of Ideas	Yes	No	Strategy	Start Date	Development of Ideas	Yes	No
1 Add detail to develop ideas fully?			9 Let the Senses Help		Add detail to develop ideas fully?		
			13 Plan It Out				
			16 Revision Strips				
			17 Rich Language Generator				
2 Use literary devices such as figurative language and imagery to convey meaning?			9 Let the Senses Help		Use literary devices such as figurative language and imagery to convey meaning?		
			16 Revision Strips				
			17 Rich Language Generator				
3 Apply strategies such as adding, deleting, substituting, and reorganizing information to revise writing?			2 Check Yourself		Apply strategies such as adding, deleting, substituting, and reorganizing information to revise writing?		
			13 Plan It Out				
			16 Revision Strips				
4 Use a variety of sentence structures to enhance writing?			5 Figurative Language Cards		Use a variety of sentence structures to enhance writing?		
			18 Sentence Search				
Voice	Yes	No	Strategy	Start Date	Voice	Yes	No
1 Match the tone of the written piece to the intended audience?			7 Give Acting a Shot		Match the tone of the written piece to the intended audience?		
			10 Listen to It				
			18 Sentence Search				
			21 Speech Bubbles				
			23 Split Voice				
			27 Transitions Book				
2 Use consistent voice throughout the written piece?			7 Give Acting a Shot		Use consistent voice throughout the written piece?		
			10 Listen to It				
			22 Spin Your Point of View				
			23 Split Voice				
			25 Three Tab POV				
3 Create voice through phrasing and the structure of the language?			7 Give Acting a Shot		Create voice through phrasing and the structure of the language?		
			9 Let the Senses Help				
			10 Listen to It				
			21 Speech Bubbles				
			23 Split Voice				
4 Engage the reader's interest?			7 Give Acting a Shot		Engage the reader's interest?		
			9 Let the Senses Help				
			10 Listen to It				
			21 Speech Bubbles				
			23 Split Voice				

	Word Choice	Yes	No	Strategy	Start Date	Word Choice	Yes	No
1	Use words appropriate for various writing purposes, such as narrative, descriptive, and expository?			12 My Main Purpose		Use words appropriate for various writing purposes, such as narrative, descriptive, and expository?		
				16 Revision Strips				
				17 Rich Language Generator				
				29 Vocabulary Line-Up				
				30 Word Stars				
2	Use verbs that are active and powerful?			9 Let the Senses Help		Use verbs that are active and powerful?		
				16 Revision Strips				
				17 Rich Language Generator				
				21 Speech Bubbles				
				29 Vocabulary Line-Up				
				30 Word Stars				
3	Use words that paint memorable pictures in the reader's mind?			9 Let the Senses Help		Use words that paint memorable pictures in the reader's mind?		
				16 Revision Strips				
				17 Rich Language Generator				
				21 Speech Bubbles				
				29 Vocabulary Line-Up				
				30 Word Stars				
	Word Choice	**Yes**	**No**	**Strategy**	**Start Date**	**Word Choice**	**Yes**	**No**
4	Use precise language to clarify ideas?			2 Check Yourself		Use precise language to clarify ideas?		
				16 Revision Strips				
				17 Rich Language Generator				
				27 Transitions Book				
				29 Vocabulary Line-Up				
				30 Word Stars				

Pretest Conventions	N/A	Good	Average	Poor
Capitalization				
At beginning of sentences				
For proper nouns				
For words that name specific people, places, or things				
Punctuation				
Commas				
Apostrophes				
Colons, semicolons				
Question marks				
Periods				
Exclamation points				
Spelling				
# of misspelled words				

Repeated misspelled words:

Presentation	N/A	Good	Average	Poor
Handwriting				
Margins				
Indentations				
Clean appearance				

Posttest Conventions	N/A	Good	Average	Poor
Capitalization				
At beginning of sentences				
For proper nouns				
For words that name specific people, places, and things				
Punctuation				
Commas				
Apostrophes				
Colons, semicolons				
Question marks				
Periods				
Exclamation points				
Spelling				
# of misspelled words				

Repeated misspelled words:

Presentation	N/A	Good	Average	Poor
Handwriting				
Margins				
Indentations				
Clean appearance				

ADDITIONAL EVALUATION INFORMATION

Student and Teacher Reflection Form

Student _____

☐ Pretest   Date: _____   ☐ Posttest   Date: _____

Essay Title: _____

Strengths of the student's essay:

Concerns about the student's essay:

☐ Focus: _____

_____

☐ Coherence: _____

_____

☐ Organization: _____

_____

☐ Development of Ideas: _____

_____

☐ Voice: _____

_____

☐ Word Choice:_____

_____

☐ Conventions:_____

_____

☐ Presentation:_____

_____

Student Reflection:

Take a moment to write about what you like most about your paper. Then write your thoughts about what your teacher discussed with you. What are some ways your teacher can help you become a better writer? What questions do you have for your teacher about writing?

APPENDIX E

Progress Monitoring Forms

TEACHER FORM: Focus

Is the Student Making Progress in the Area of Focus?

Student: _____ Date: _____

I. Before the student writes . . .

1. Record the topic the student is writing about: _____

_____

_____

2. Check the areas of instruction that have been completed prior to the student completing the writing sample.

Classroom Instruction Before This Writing Sample	Focus Strategies Used Before This Writing Sample
☐ Focus	☐ Strategy 1 : 3-2-1
☐ Coherence	☐ Strategy 2: Check Yourself
☐ Organization	☐ Strategy 4: Editing Irrelevant Information
☐ Development of Ideas	☐ Strategy 7: Give Acting a Shot
☐ Voice	☐ Strategy 11: Magnifying Glass
☐ Word Choice	☐ Strategy 12: My Main Purpose
☐ Convention	☐ Strategy 14: Prewriting Pyramid
☐ Presentation	☐ Strategy 15: Questions to Clarify
☐ Other:	☐ Strategy 20: Soccer, Anyone?
	☐ Strategy 24: Stick to the Point
	☐ Strategy 26: Topic Sentence Development
	☐ None; this is the first writing sample.

II. After the student completes the writing sample . . .

1. Record the title of the essay: _____

_____

_____

2. Look for evidence of focus:

	Yes	No
a. Did the student have a clear understanding of the audience?	☐	☐
b. Did the student have a clear purpose for writing about the topic?	☐	☐
c. Did the student have a well-developed topic sentence?	☐	☐
d. Did the student's main points support the topic sentence?	☐	☐
e. Did the student include little irrelevant information?	☐	☐

3. Conference with the student. Describe the strengths of the writing sample and associated concerns. Date of Conference: _____

4. Notes for the conference:

5. Inform the student that the following strategies will be applied in class to enhance the skill of focus:

☐ Strategy 1: 3-2-1	☐ Strategy 14: Prewriting Pyramid
☐ Strategy 2: Check Yourself	☐ Strategy 15: Questions to Clarify
☐ Strategy 4: Editing Irrelevant Information	☐ Strategy 20: Soccer, Anyone?
☐ Strategy 7: Give Acting a Shot	☐ Strategy 24: Stick to the Point
☐ Strategy 11: Magnifying Glass	☐ Strategy 26: Topic Sentence Development
☐ Strategy 12: My Main Purpose	☐ None; the student has mastered the trait of focus.

6. Keep this form in the student's writing portfolio. After applying the strategies, acquire another writing sample from the same student. Alternatively, the student can rewrite this evaluated piece. Use a new Progress Monitoring Form. Assemble all of the forms in chronological order. This will help you monitor the student's progress toward improving the skill of focus.

STUDENT FORM: Focus

Are You Making Progress in the Area of Focus?

Name: _____ Date: _____

Title: _____

Your teacher is evaluating the focus of your writing. As you write, pay close attention to the following focus characteristics:

☐ I have a clear purpose for writing about the topic.

☐ Main points in my sentences relate to the topic sentence.

☐ I have a topic sentence that represents what I want to say.

☐ I only include relevant information.

Focus Strategies I Used:

☐ 3-2-1

☐ Prewriting Pyramid

☐ Check Yourself

☐ Questions to Clarify

☐ Editing Irrelevant Information

☐ Soccer, Anyone?

☐ Give Acting a Shot

☐ Stick to the Point

☐ Magnifying Glass

☐ Topic Sentence Development

☐ My Main Purpose

☐ None

Write your essay/composition here and continue on the back:

Write one sentence about what you like most about your writing sample:

Keep this form in your writing portfolio. Assemble all of the focus forms in chronological order. This will help you monitor your own progress toward improving the skill of focus.

TEACHER FORM: Coherence

Is the Student Making Progress in the Area of Coherence?

Student: _____ Date: _____

I. Before the student writes . . .

1. Record the topic the student is writing about: _____

_____

_____

2. Check the areas of instruction that have been completed prior to the student completing the writing sample.

Classroom Instruction Before This Writing Sample	Coherence Strategies Used Before This Writing Sample
☐ Focus	☐ Strategy 1: 3-2-1
☐ Coherence	☐ Strategy 2: Check Yourself
☐ Organization	☐ Strategy 3: Color Coding for Consistency
☐ Development of Ideas	☐ Strategy 6: Flying High
☐ Voice	☐ Strategy 8: Graphic Organizers
☐ Word Choice	☐ Strategy 15: Questions to Clarify
☐ Convention	☐ Strategy 19: Sequence Cards
☐ Presentation	☐ Strategy 20: Soccer, Anyone?
☐ Other:	☐ Strategy 22: Spin Your Point of View
	☐ Strategy 25: Three Tab POV
	☐ Strategy 27: Transitions Book
	☐ None; this is the first writing sample.

II. After the student completes the writing sample . . .

1. Record the title of the essay:_____

2. Look for evidence of coherence:

	Yes	No
a. Did the student group related sentences within paragraphs?	☐	☐
b. Did the student group related ideas into separate paragraphs?	☐	☐
c. Did the student convey a consistent point of view throughout the written piece?	☐	☐
d. Did the student add supporting details that align with the focus?	☐	☐

3. Conference with the student. Describe the strengths of the writing sample and associated concerns. Date of Conference:_____

4. Notes for the conference:

5. Inform the student that the following strategies will be applied in class to enhance the skill of coherence:

☐ Strategy 1: 3-2-1	☐ Strategy 19: Sequence Cards
☐ Strategy 2: Check Yourself	☐ Strategy 20: Soccer, Anyone?
☐ Strategy 3: Color Coding for Consistency	☐ Strategy 22: Spin Your Point of View
☐ Strategy 6: Flying High	☐ Strategy 25: Three Tab POV
☐ Strategy 8: Graphic Organizers	☐ Strategy 27: Transitions Book
☐ Strategy 15: Questions to Clarify	☐ None; the student has mastered the trait of coherence.

6. Keep this form in the student's writing portfolio. After applying the strategies, acquire another writing sample from the same student. Alternatively, the student can rewrite this evaluated piece. Use a new Progress Monitoring Form. Assemble all of the forms in chronological order. This will help you monitor the student's progress toward improving the skill of coherence.

STUDENT FORM: Coherence

Are You Making Progress in the Area of Coherence?

Name: _____ Date: _____

Title: _____

Your teacher is evaluating the coherence of your writing. As you write, pay close attention to the following coherence characteristics:

☐ I group my related sentences within paragraphs.

☐ I group my related ideas into separate paragraphs.

☐ I have a consistent point of view throughout my essay.

☐ I add supporting details that align with my focus.

Coherence Strategies I Used:

☐ 3-2-1

☐ Check Yourself

☐ Color Coding for Consistency

☐ Flying High

☐ Graphic Organizers

☐ Questions to Clarify

☐ Sequence Cards

☐ Soccer, Anyone?

☐ Spin Your Point of View

☐ Three Tab POV

☐ Transitions Book

☐ None

Write your essay/composition here and continue on the back:

Write one sentence about what you like most about your writing sample:

Keep this form in your writing portfolio. Assemble all of the coherence forms in chronological order. This will help you monitor your own progress toward improving the skill of coherence.

TEACHER FORM: Organization

Is the Student Making Progress in the Area of Organization?

Student: _____ Date: _____

I. Before the student writes . . .

1. Record the topic the student is writing about:

_____

_____

2. Check the areas of instruction that have been completed prior to the student completing the writing sample.

Classroom Instruction Before This Writing Sample	Organization Strategies Used Before This Writing Sample
☐ Focus	☐ Strategy 6: Flying High
☐ Coherence	☐ Strategy 8: Graphic Organizers
☐ Organization	☐ Strategy 12: My Main Purpose
☐ Development of Ideas	☐ Strategy 13: Plan It Out
☐ Voice	☐ Strategy 14: Prewriting Pyramid
☐ Word Choice	☐ Strategy 15: Questions to Clarify
☐ Convention	☐ Strategy 19: Sequence Cards
☐ Presentation	☐ Strategy 20: Soccer, Anyone?
☐ Other:	☐ Strategy 22: Spin Your Point of View
	☐ Strategy 23: Split Voice
	☐ Strategy 27: Transitions Book
	☐ Strategy 28: Transitions Spinner
	☐ None; this is the first writing sample.

II. After the student completes the writing sample . . .

1. Record the title of the essay:

_____

_____

2. Look for evidence of organization:

	Yes	No
a. Did the student use effective prewriting strategies such as webs, timelines, or outlines?	☐	☐
b. Did the student apply transitions to guide the reader through the written piece?	☐	☐
c. Did the student organize writing in a logical sequence around a central idea?	☐	☐
d. Did the student arrange ideas to convey meaning through use of strategies such as chronology, cause and effect, and compare and contrast?	☐	☐

3. Conference with the student. Describe the strengths of the writing sample and associated concerns. Date of Conference: _____

4. Notes for the conference:

5. Inform the student that the following strategies will be applied in class to enhance the skill of organization:

☐ Strategy 6: Flying High	☐ Strategy 20: Soccer, Anyone?
☐ Strategy 8: Graphic Organizers	☐ Strategy 22: Spin Your Point of View
☐ Strategy 12: My Main Purpose	☐ Strategy 23: Split Voice
☐ Strategy 13: Plan It Out	☐ Strategy 27: Transitions Book
☐ Strategy 14: Prewriting Pyramid	☐ Strategy 28: Transitions Spinner
☐ Strategy 15: Questions to Clarify	☐ None; the student has mastered the trait of
☐ Strategy 19: Sequence Cards	organization.

6. Keep this form in the student's writing portfolio. After applying the strategies, acquire another writing sample from the same student. Alternatively, the student can rewrite this evaluated piece. Use a new Progress Monitoring Form. Assemble all of the forms in chronological order. This will help you monitor the student's progress toward improving the skill of organization.

STUDENT FORM: Organization

Are You Making Progress in the Area of Organization?

Name: _____ Date: _____

Title: _____

Your teacher is evaluating the organization of your writing. As you write, pay close attention to the following organization characteristics:

☐ I use prewriting strategies such as webs, timelines, and outlines.

☐ I apply transition words to guide the reader through my essay.

☐ I organize my essay in logical order around my topic.

☐ I arrange my ideas so they have meaning by using strategies such as chronology, cause and effect, and compare and contrast.

Organization Strategies I Used:

☐ Flying High
☐ Graphic Organizers
☐ My Main Purpose
☐ Plan It Out
☐ Prewriting Pyramid
☐ Questions to Clarify

☐ Sequence Cards
☐ Soccer, Anyone?
☐ Spin Your Point of View
☐ Split Voice
☐ Transitions Book
☐ None

Write your essay/composition here and continue on the back:

Write one sentence about what you like most about your writing sample:

Keep this form in your writing portfolio. Assemble all of the organization forms in chronological order. This will help you monitor your own progress toward improving the skill of organization.

TEACHER FORM: Development of Ideas

Is the Student Making Progress in the Area of Development of Ideas?

Student: _____ Date: _____

I. Before the student writes . . .

1. Record the topic the student is writing about:

_____

_____

2. Check the areas of instruction that have been completed prior to the student completing the writing sample.

Classroom Instruction Before This Writing Sample	Development of Ideas Strategies Used Before This Writing Sample
☐ Focus	☐ Strategy 2: Check Yourself
☐ Coherence	☐ Strategy 5: Figurative Language Cards
☐ Organization	☐ Strategy 9: Let the Senses Help
☐ Development of Ideas	☐ Strategy 13: Plan It Out
☐ Voice	☐ Strategy 16: Revision Strips
☐ Word Choice	☐ Strategy 17: Rich Language Generator
☐ Convention	☐ Strategy 18: Sentence Search
☐ Presentation	☐ None; this is the first writing sample.
☐ Other:	

II. After the student completes the writing sample . . .

1. Record the title of the essay:

_____

_____

2. Look for evidence of development of ideas:

	Yes	No
a. Did the student add details to fully develop ideas?	☐	☐
b. Did the student use literary devices such as figurative language and imagery to convey meaning?	☐	☐
c. Did the student apply strategies such as adding, deleting, substituting, and reorganizing information to revise writing?	☐	☐
d. Did the student use a variety of sentence structures to enhance writing?	☐	☐

3. Conference with the student. Describe the strengths of the writing sample and associated concerns. Date of Conference: _____

4. Notes for the conference:

5. Inform the student that the following strategies will be applied in class to enhance the skill of development of ideas:

☐ Strategy 2: Check Yourself	☐ Strategy 16: Revision Strips
☐ Strategy 5: Figurative Language Cards	☐ Strategy 17: Rich Language Generator
☐ Strategy 9: Let the Senses Help	☐ Strategy 18: Sentence Search
☐ Strategy 13: Plan It Out	☐ None; the student has mastered the trait of development of ideas.

6. Keep this form in the student's writing portfolio. After applying the strategies, acquire another writing sample from the same student. Alternatively, the student can rewrite this evaluated piece. Use a new Progress Monitoring Form. Assemble all of the forms in chronological order. This will help you monitor the student's progress toward improving the skill of development of ideas.

STUDENT FORM: Development of Ideas

Are You Making Progress in the Area of Development of Ideas?

Name:_____ Date:_____

Title:_____

Your teacher is evaluating the development of ideas in your writing. As you write, pay close attention to the following development of ideas characteristics:

☐ I add detail to fully develop my ideas.

☐ I use figurative language and imagery so that my essay has meaning.

☐ I use strategies such as adding, deleting, substituting, and reorganizing information.

☐ I use different types of sentence structures to enhance writing.

Development of Ideas Strategies I Used:

☐ Check Yourself

☐ Figurative Language Cards

☐ Let the Senses Help

☐ Plan It Out

☐ Revision Strips

☐ Rich Language Generator

☐ Sentence Search

☐ None

Write your essay/composition here and continue on the back:

Write one sentence about what you like most about your writing sample:

Keep this form in your writing portfolio. Assemble all of the development of ideas forms in chronological order. This will help you monitor your own progress toward improving the skill of development of ideas.

TEACHER FORM: Voice

Is the Student Making Progress in the Area of Voice?

Student: _____ Date: _____

I. Before the student writes . . .

1. Record the topic the student is writing about:

_____

_____

2. Check the areas of instruction that have been completed prior to the student completing the writing sample.

Classroom Instruction Before This Writing Sample	Voice Strategies Used Before This Writing Sample
☐ Focus	☐ Strategy 7: Give Acting a Shot
☐ Coherence	☐ Strategy 9: Let the Senses Help
☐ Organization	☐ Strategy 10: Listen To It
☐ Development of Ideas	☐ Strategy 18: Sentence Search
☐ Voice	☐ Strategy 21: Speech Bubbles
☐ Word Choice	☐ Strategy 22: Spin Your Point of View
☐ Convention	☐ Strategy 23: Split Voice
☐ Presentation	☐ Strategy 25: Three Tab POV
☐ Other:	☐ Strategy 27: Transitions Book
	☐ None; this is the first writing sample.

II. After the student completes the writing sample . . .

1. Record the title of the essay:

_____

_____

2. Look for evidence of voice:

	Yes	No
a. Did the student match the tone of the written piece to the intended audience?	☐	☐
b. Did the student use consistent voice throughout the written piece?	☐	☐
c. Did the student create voice through phrasing and language structure?	☐	☐
d. Did the student engage the reader's interest?	☐	☐

3. Conference with the student. Describe the strengths of the writing sample and associated concerns. Date of Conference: _____

4. Notes for the conference:

5. Inform the student that the following strategies will be applied in class to enhance the skill of voice:

☐ Strategy 7: Give Acting a Shot	☐ Strategy 22: Spin Your Point of View
☐ Strategy 9: Let the Senses Help	☐ Strategy 23: Split Voice
☐ Strategy 10: Listen To It	☐ Strategy 25: Three Tab POV
☐ Strategy 18: Sentence Search	☐ Strategy 27: Transitions Book
☐ Strategy 21: Speech Bubbles	☐ None; the student has mastered the trait of voice.

6. Keep this form in the student's writing portfolio. After applying the strategies, acquire another writing sample from the same student. Alternatively, the student can rewrite this evaluated piece. Use a new Progress Monitoring Form. Assemble all of the forms in chronological order. This will help you monitor the student's progress toward improving the skill of voice.

STUDENT FORM: Voice

Are You Making Progress in the Area of Voice?

Name: _____ Date: _____

Title: _____

Your teacher is evaluating the voice of your writing. As you write, pay close attention to the following voice characteristics:

☐ I match the tone of my essay to my audience.

☐ I use a consistent voice throughout my essay.

☐ I create a unique voice by using phrases and language that demonstrate my feelings.

☐ I engage my reader's interest.

Voice Strategies I Used:

☐ Give Acting a Shot

☐ Let the Senses Help

☐ Listen To It

☐ Sentence Search

☐ Speech Bubbles

☐ Spin Your Point of View

☐ Split Voice

☐ Three Tab POV

☐ Transitions Book

☐ None

Write your essay/composition here and continue on the back:

Write one sentence about what you like most about your writing sample:

Keep this form in your writing portfolio. Assemble all of the voice forms in chronological order. This will help you monitor your own progress toward improving the skill of voice.

TEACHER FORM: Word Choice

Is the Student Making Progress in the Area of Word Choice?

Student: _____ Date: _____

I. Before the student writes . . .

1. Record the topic the student is writing about:

_____

_____

2. Check the areas of instruction that have been completed prior to the student completing the writing sample.

Classroom Instruction Before This Writing Sample	Word Choice Strategies Used Before This Writing Sample
☐ Focus	☐ Strategy 2: Check Yourself
☐ Coherence	☐ Strategy 9: Let the Senses Help
☐ Organization	☐ Strategy 12: My Main Purpose
☐ Development of Ideas	☐ Strategy 16: Revision Strips
☐ Voice	☐ Strategy 17: Rich Language Generator
☐ Word Choice	☐ Strategy 21: Speech Bubbles
☐ Convention	☐ Strategy 27: Transitions Book
☐ Presentation	☐ Strategy 29: Vocabulary Line-Up
☐ Other:	☐ Strategy 30: Word Stars
	☐ None; this is the first writing sample.

II. After the student completes the writing sample . . .

1. Record the title of the essay:

_____

_____

2. Look for evidence of word choice:

	Yes	No
a. Did the student use words appropriate for various writing purposes such as narrative, descriptive, and expository?	☐	☐
b. Did the student use verbs that are active and powerful?	☐	☐
c. Did the student use words that paint memorable pictures in the reader's mind?	☐	☐
d. Did the student use precise language to clarify ideas?	☐	☐

3. Conference with the student. Describe the strengths of the writing sample and associated concerns. Date of Conference:_____

4. Notes for the conference:

5. Inform the student that the following strategies will be applied in class to enhance the skill of word choice:

☐ Strategy 3: Check Yourself	☐ Strategy 21: Speech Bubbles
☐ Strategy 9: Let the Senses Help	☐ Strategy 27: Transitions Book
☐ Strategy 12: My Main Purpose	☐ Strategy 29: Vocabulary Line-Up
☐ Strategy 16: Revision Strips	☐ Strategy 30: Word Stars
☐ Strategy 17: Rich Language Generator	☐ None; the student has mastered the trait of word choice.

6. Keep this form in the student's writing portfolio. After applying the strategies, acquire another writing sample from the same student. Alternatively, the student can rewrite this evaluated piece. Use a new Progress Monitoring Form. Assemble all of the forms in chronological order. This will help you monitor the student's progress toward improving the skill of word choice.

STUDENT FORM: Word Choice

Are You Making Progress in the Area of Word Choice?

Name: _____ Date: _____

Title: _____

Your teacher is evaluating word choice in your writing. As you write, pay close attention to the following word choice characteristics:

☐ I use words appropriate for the purpose (narrative, descriptive, and expository).

☐ I use active and powerful verbs.

☐ I use words that paint pictures in the minds of my readers.

☐ I use precise language to make my ideas clear.

Word Choice Strategies I Used:

☐ Check Yourself

☐ Let the Senses Help

☐ My Main Purpose

☐ Revision Strips

☐ Rich Language Generator

☐ Speech Bubbles

☐ Transitions Book

☐ Vocabulary Line-Up

☐ Word Stars

☐ None

Write your essay/composition here and continue on the back:

Write one sentence about what you like most about your writing sample:

Keep this form in your writing portfolio. Assemble all of the word choice forms in chronological order. This will help you monitor your own progress toward improving the skill of word choice.

APPENDIX F

RESOURCES FOR PARENTS

Included in this appendix are two resources of the toolbox that are for parents. The first is a letter that explains the evaluation process, and the other is a handout that describes the eight writing traits and includes suggested activities that can be done at home to promote writing. Send these resources home to parents with copies of their child's essay and respective evaluation protocol so they can gain a better understanding of the writing traits and how the strategies work to maximize their child's writing performance.

Letter to Parents

Dear Parents,

As you know, writing is such an important part of communication, and I am working hard to maximize your child's writing performance. Recently, _____ wrote an essay in response to a prompt to help me identify his/her writing strengths as well as areas that still need work.

I've included a copy of _____'s essay and a form that describes my evaluation of his/her essay. I've checked the areas that I plan to develop in class. I'm including a description of those areas so you can spend some time reinforcing the skills that need further development.

In the next few months, I will reassess _____'s writing with a different writing prompt and will send home the results of his/her writing achievement.

Thank you,

The Writing Traits: Strategies for Parents

Trait #1 Focus	Trait #2 Coherence	Trait #3 Organization
Focus is the central idea or controlling theme of a piece of writing. It's also known as "sticking to the point." Student writers achieve clear focus when they know what they want to write and how they want to write about it.	Coherence refers to the connection of ideas that support the focus. Effective student writers order their ideas so that each sentence and paragraph logically connects to the controlling theme.	Organization is evident when the essay or story is written in a fashion that makes sense. Ideas are linked logically from sentence to sentence and from paragraph to paragraph.
Characteristics of Focus • There is a clear understanding of the audience. • There is a clear purpose for writing. The writer understands and demonstrates his or her reason for writing about the topic. • There is one controlling theme. • The main points are clear. • Writers can choose a close-up, narrow perspective or a broad, wide-range perspective.	*Characteristics of Coherence* • Coherence exists within paragraphs (sentence to sentence) and among paragraphs (paragraph to paragraph). • The supporting details align with the focus. • Each part contributes to the whole piece of writing. • There are no shifts in ideas that render gaps in a reader's understanding. • There is a sense of completeness.	*Characteristics of Organization* • There is evidence of an organizational strategy. • There is a meaningful introduction and conclusion. • There are strong and meaningful transitions. • Information is conveyed in a manner that makes sense.
Sample Activities for Home ✓ Define *main point* in your own words (e.g., explain the main point of books or stories that you read together, the main point of a TV show, the main point of a familiar story, etc.). ✓ Define *controlling theme* in your own words (e.g., use the themes of familiar stories). ✓ Define *purpose* (e.g., have your child explain the purpose of writing a story, the purpose of explaining how to do something, etc.). ✓ Ask your child to describe items from a close-up (like the TV remote) and a broad perspective (like the TV and furniture up against the wall). Have your child explain the differences between the two.	*Sample Activities for Home* ✓ Give your child one main point and have him or her describe several details that support it (e.g., ice cream is a good dessert; ice cream is a healthy dairy product; ice cream can have natural fruits; etc.). ✓ Explain how TV shows, songs, and books often have parts that contribute to one controlling thought. Tell your child how good writers generally do not stray from that one thought. ✓ Use a familiar story to show how good stories have a sense of completeness (i.e., how each part connects to one controlling theme).	*Sample Activities for Home* ✓ Explain to your child how good pieces of writing have a meaningful introduction, middle, and conclusion. Emphasize how TV shows often try to "hook" viewers with an interesting introduction. Provide them with some examples. ✓ Explain that your child's writing should group sentences and paragraphs in such a way that it makes logical sense to readers. ✓ Explain that the best way to have effective transitions is to organize ideas before writing so that all of the paragraphs support the one controlling theme.

Have your child write a story. Ask him or her to explain how the story demonstrates focus, coherence, and organization.

Trait #4	Trait #5	Trait #6
Development of Ideas	**Voice**	**Word Choice**
Writers deepen their readers' understanding of the work through ideas that reveal depth of thought and substance.	Voice is what makes a writer's style unique. Convictions and feelings are evident through the writer's choice of words.	A good writer uses rich and precise language in a functional way that enlightens and engages the reader. Strong word choice can expand and clarify ideas, create strong images that connect the reader to the writing, and guide the reader to a new understanding of the topic.
Characteristics of Development of Ideas • The writer uses literary devices—such as figurative language, imagery, suspense, and dialogue—effectively. • The writer adds, deletes, combines, and rearranges sentences and details to elaborate on his or her ideas. • The writer effectively uses sentence variety (e.g., length and structure, rhythm, cadence, fragments, compound, compound/complex, simple, etc.).	*Characteristics of Voice* • The writer's voice is authentic and engages the reader. • The writing demonstrates that the writer cares about the topic. • There is a unique perspective. • The writer's voice is based on an understanding of his or her purpose and audience. • The writer uses two modes of voice: active (the subject is the doer) and passive (the subject is the receiver of the action). • Enhanced vocabulary, such as the effective use of vivid verbs (e.g., *strong*, *striking*, *energetic*, *active*), is used throughout the writing.	*Characteristics of Word Choice* • The writer chooses the right words and phrases for the mode of writing (e.g., descriptive, narrative, persuasive). • The writer uses words and phrases to create meaning and engage the reader. • The writer strategically places words and phrases for a desired emphasis. • The writer uses words and phrases for originality. • The writer uses connotative and/or denotative words. • The writer uses active verbs.

The Writing Traits: Strategies for Parents *(continued)*

Trait #4	Trait #5	Trait #6
Development of Ideas	**Voice**	**Word Choice**
Sample Activities for Home	*Sample Activities for Home*	*Sample Activities for Home*
✓ Have your child explain how to improve a simple sentence using figurative language. For example, "The boy went to the store" can be adapted to "The red-headed boy raced swiftly to the local grocer eager to buy chocolate." "The girl was scared" can be adapted to "She paused. She took a hard swallow. She didn't dare blink because she was as frightened as can be." ✓ Identify common objects at home, such as the toaster, refrigerator, and alarm clock, and have your child think of details that make them more interesting. For example, "The rackety old toaster, as noisy as can be, still works!" Alternatively, "That trusty, strikingly white refrigerator keeps our food crisp and fresh."	✓ Have your child use vivid verbs at home. For instance, "Mom *embraces* us every morning" "I *saunter* to my room," and "The trees *sway* softly in the wind." ✓ Explain active voice: "The baby is eating her food." "Karen drove the car." "We were sad that the show was canceled." "Dad will drive you to soccer practice." Have your child come up with some examples of his or her own. ✓ Explain passive voice: "The food is being eaten by the baby." "The car was driven by Karen." "You will be driven to soccer practice." Have your child come up with some examples of his or her own.	✓ Come up with as many synonyms as possible for common words your child uses. For instance, instead of *happy*, consider *content*, *jolly*, *joyful*, or *thrilled*. Keep these in a child-made dictionary, index cards, or a special notebook. ✓ Pick a word, such as *sad*, and come up with an alternative word. Tell your child that he or she has to guess the other word. For instance, say, "I'm thinking of a word similar to *sad*. Can you guess the word?" Your child might respond with "*Bitter? Depressed? Heartbroken?*" and so forth until he or she guesses your word.
Have your child write a story. Ask him or her to explain how the story demonstrates development of ideas, voice, and word choice.		

Trait #7	Trait #8
Conventions	**Presentation**
The term *conventions* refers to the mechanics of writing—spelling, punctuation, capitalization, grammar/usage, and paragraphing. Students who understand the conventions spell high-frequency words correctly; apply standard spelling strategies; apply structural aspects of phonemes, diphthongs, and so forth; and use punctuation and capitalization rules effectively.	Presentation refers to the appearance of the essay in actual form, on paper. Essays that demonstrate good presentation look neat.
Characteristics of Conventions	*Characteristics of Presentation*
• The writer knows the punctuation rules associated with each of the four kinds of sentences. • The writer uses the comma, the colon, the semicolon, quotation marks, and the apostrophe correctly. • The writer knows there are rules that predict a general structure of spelling. • The writer knows there are words that do not follow typical spelling rules. • The writer uses mnemonic devices and other strategies to develop his or her spelling ability. • The writer recognizes and corrects run-on sentences. • There is subject-verb agreement in the writer's written work. • The writer uses verb tenses correctly.	• The writer uses a heading that fulfills the standards of the district. • The writer uses appropriately sized margins. • The writer uses minimal smears and/or traces of eraser marks. • The writer uses few (or no) deletion and insertion marks. • The writer uses—if appropriate—graphics that complement the essay.
Sample Activities for Home	*Sample Activities for Home*
✓ Explain when to use a comma, period, question mark, and exclamation point correctly. ✓ Explain when to use a colon, a semicolon, quotation marks, and an apostrophe correctly. ✓ Write some spelling rules, such as '*i* before *e* except after *c*,' on index cards with some appropriate and relevant words. ✓ Write words that do not have common spelling rules on separate index cards (e.g., *colonel, debt, knob, align,* etc.).	✓ Explain what an essay with a neat appearance looks like.
Have your child write a story. Ask him or her to explain how the story demonstrates good use of conventions and has a nice presentation.	

REFERENCES

Bellamy, R. C. (n.d.). *Research on writing with the 6+1 traits.* Retrieved from http://educationnorthwest.org/webfm_send/143

Center for Curriculum Renewal. (n.d.). *Development of common assessments: A design overview.* Retrieved from http://curriculumrenewal.com

Chenoweth, K. (2009). *How it's being done: Urgent lessons from unexpected school.* Cambridge, MA: Harvard Education Press.

Christman, J. B., Neild, R. C., Bulkley, K., Blanc, S., Liu, R., Mitchell, C., & Travers, E. (2009). *Making the most of interim assessment data: Lessons from Philadelphia.* Philadelphia: Research for Action.

Common Core State Standards Initiative. (2013). *English language arts standards, writing, 5th grade.* Retrieved from www.corestandards.org/ELA-Literacy/W/5

Cooper, J. D., & Kiger, N. D. (2006). *Literacy: Helping children construct meaning.* Boston: Houghton Mifflin.

Dudley-Marling, C., & Paugh, P. C. (2009). *A classroom teacher's guide to struggling writers: How to provide differentiated support and ongoing assessment.* Retrieved from www.heinemann.com/shared/onlineresources/E00765/Dudley00765Sample.pdf

Graham, S. (2013). *It all starts here: Fixing our national writing crisis from the foundation.* Retrieved from www.zaner-bloser.com/media/zb/zaner-bloser/pdf/C3316_It_All_Starts_Here.pdf

Hammill, D. D., & Larsen, S. C. (2009). *Test of written language* (3rd ed.). Austin, TX: Pro-Ed, Inc.

Higgins, B., Miller, M., & Wegmann, S. (2007). Teaching to the test . . . not! Balancing test practices and testing requirements in writing. *Reading Teacher, 60*(4), 310–390.

Jarmer, D., Kozol, M., Nelson, S., & Salsberry, T. (2000). Six-trait writing model improves scores at Jennie Wilson Elementary. *Journal of School Improvement, 1*(2), 29–32.

King, T. (2012). *Common assessments and ELLs.* Retrieved from http://widaatwcer.blogspot.com/2012/03/common-assessments-and-ells.html

Lienemann, T. O., & Reid, R. (2008). Using self-regulated strategy development to improve expository writing with students with attention deficit hyperactivity disorder. *Exceptional Children, 74*(4), 471–486.

Martin, R. A. (2006). Wake-up call brings a jolt of alignment to the curriculum. *National Staff Development Council, 27*(1), 53–55.

National Center for Education Statistics. (2012). *The nation's report card: Writing 2011* (NCES 2012-470). Institute of Education Sciences, U.S. Department of Education, Washington, D.C.

National Center on Response to Intervention. (2010, March). *Essential components of RTI: A closer look at response to intervention.* Washington, DC: U.S. Department of Education, Office of Special Education Programs, National Center on Response to Intervention.

National Council of Teachers of English. (1996). *Standards for the English language arts.* Retrieved from www.ncte.org/library/NCTEFiles/Resources/Books/Sample/StandardsDoc.pdf

Northwest Regional Educational Laboratory. (2012). *6 + 1 Traits definitions.* Retrieved from http://educationnorthwest.org/resource/503

Reeves, D. B. (2004). *Accountability for learning: How teachers and leaders can take charge.* Alexandria, VA: ASCD.

Schmoker, M. (2004). Learning communities at the crossroads: Toward the best schools we've ever had. *Phi Delta Kappan, 86*(1), 84–88.

Spandel, V., & Stiggins, R. (1997). *Creating writers: Linking writing assessment and instruction.* New York: Longman.

Whitten, E., Esteves, K. J., & Woodrow, A. (2009). *RTI success: Proven tools and strategies for schools and classrooms.* Minneapolis, MN: Free Spirit.

Williams, J., Homan, E. C., & Swofford, S. (2011). *Supporting students in a time of core standards: English language arts grades 3–5.* Urbana, IL: National Council of Teachers of English.

Index

ABOUT THE AUTHORS

David Campos began his career in education over 20 years ago when he started teaching 2nd grade. He later entered graduate school, taught ESL, and worked in corporate training and development. He earned his Ph.D. from The University of Texas at Austin, specializing in learning disabilities and behavior disorders. His first job in academia was at Roosevelt University (Chicago), where he was an assistant professor in the College of Education. After earning rank and tenure, he became an associate professor of education at the University of the Incarnate Word, where he has supervised student teachers and taught undergraduate and graduate courses in special education, multicultural education, and instructional design and delivery.

David has written books focused on English language learners, childhood obesity, and gay and lesbian youth. He was guest editor of a special issue of the *Journal of Hispanic Higher Education*, which focused on language acquisition as it relates to Latino students. His peer-reviewed articles focus on constructivist teaching and authentic assessment by way of African American visionaries. David spends his time between San Antonio, Austin, and his parents' lake home outside Marble Fall, Texas.

Kathleen Fad is an author and consultant from Austin, Texas. Kathy's professional experience has spanned over 30 years as a general education teacher, special education teacher, university professor, author, and independent consultant. Kathy's specialty is designing practical, common-sense strategies that are research based. Kathy has coauthored numerous books, articles, and assessment instruments. The *Practical Ideas That Really Work* series now includes a wide variety of topics, such as ADHD, autism, disruptive behaviors, reading problems, and giftedness. Kathy's latest book includes interventions for students with high-functioning autism.

Kathy's staff development often relates to differentiated instructional strategies, collaboration, and RTI interventions that impact both academics and behavior. With a Master's degree and Ph.D. in special education, as well as teaching and consulting experience in general education, Kathy's work with inclusionary and coteaching instructional arrangements has been a great fit for her skills. Specialties in autism and emotional disturbance have also given her perspective and expertise with challenging situations that teachers and administrators face. Kathy often works with beginning teachers and schools that are working to maintain effective student intervention teams and implement Tier 2 and Tier 3 academic or behavioral interventions. Kathy's website, Tools for Great Teachers, can be found at www.toolsforgreatteachers.com.

Related ASCD Resources

At the time of publication, the following ASCD resources were available (ASCD stock numbers appear in parentheses). For up-to-date information about ASCD resources, go to www.ascd.org. You can search the complete archives of Educational Leadership at http://www.ascd.org/el.

ASCD EDge©

Exchange ideas and connect with other educators on the social networking site ASCD Edge at http://ascdedge.ascd.org/

Print Products

Classroom Instruction That Works: Research-Based Strategies for Increasing Student Achievement (2nd Ed) by Ceri B. Dean, Elizabeth Ross Hubbell, Howard Pitler, and Bj Stone (#111001)

Essential Questions: Opening Doors to Student Understanding by Jay McTighe and Grant Wiggins (#109004)

How to Differentiate Instruction in Mixed-Ability Classrooms (2nd Ed) by Carol Ann Tomlinson (#101043)

Read, Write, Lead: Breakthrough Strategies for Schoolwide Literacy Success by Regie Routman (#113016)

Teaching Writing in the Content Areas by Vicki Urquhart and Monette McIver (#105036)

THE WHOLE CHILD The Whole Child Initiative helps schools and communities create learning environments that allow students to be healthy, safe, engaged, supported, and challenged. To learn more about other books and resources that relate to the whole child, visit www.wholechildeducation.org.

For more information: send e-mail to member@ascd.org; call 1-800-933-2723 or 703-578-9600, press 2; send a fax to 703-575-5400; or write to Information Services, ASCD, 1703 N. Beauregard St., Alexandria, VA 22311-1714 USA.